IS YOUR SMARTPHONE YOUR **POSSESSION** OR YOUR **OBSESSION?**

 WARNING
If You Read This Book,
You May Get
Red Pilled

-JACK WEDAM-

Printed in the United States of America

Library of Congress Control Number: 2019920991
ISBN: Softcover   978-1-64376-738-3
            Hardback   978-1-64376-739-0
            eBook   978-1-64376-737-6

Republished by: PageTurner, Press and Media LLC
Publication Date: 02/12/2020

To order copies of this book, contact:

PageTurner, Press and Media
Phone: 1-888-447-9651
order@pageturner.us
www.pageturner.us

Contents

Preface

I have been concerned for many years about how smartphones and other smart devices influence people. While many fawning journalists and writers are trying to outdo one another by pouring lavish praise upon tech companies and tech billionaires, I called them out in my previous books for what they are really doing.

It was not good for my book sales. However, it was a great opportunity for establishing my credibility.

Many journalists and writers have written about smartphone addiction. However, no one else has tried tracing the addiction back to the Central Intelligence Agency that funded research into dopamine as part of MKULTRA[a] mind control and behavior modification projects.[2] Dopamine is part of the reward pleasure pathway in the brain. Dopamine is responsible for the addictive power of cocaine, amphetamines, and other drugs. Many former insiders from big tech companies acknowledge that they deliberately designed smartphones and many apps including Facebook to release dopamine in people's brains.

I dug up many facts that other authors would not write about. Perhaps they did not know where to look. Maybe they could not invest the effort to dig up the underlying facts. Perhaps they were under the spell of the Mighty Wurlitzer[3] (or some reincarnation of it). Maybe they were afraid to report what they found.

In the course of my previous work, I was privy to information

---

a   The CIA started UKULTRA several decades ago as a mind control and behavior modification program. Research using drugs as a method of mind control and behavior modification allegedly was terminated by the 1970s. Other programs that did not use drugs may have continued. Several recent patents on manipulating the brain and nervous suggests the research was transformed into usable technology. *Brainwashing* and *MKULTRA* were referenced several times in one patent that alleges a computer program can *influence* people toward a *desired outcome*.

that few others could see. That experience caused me to ask myself, "What else is there? What else is going on?" After extensive research, I eventually found and dug up many of the answers in open sources materials.

It amazed me "what else" I discovered. This book is not a conspiracy theory. It is thoroughly documented, as you can see, by examining the endnotes.

I discovered that there was a tremendous treasure trove of information hiding in plain sight. Consider a wild animal with its natural camouflage lying still in its natural habitat. It is hard to see the wild animal unless you know what to look for and someone points out where to look. What may initially look like conspiracy theories in this book are not conspiracy ones at all. All my assertions—as audacious as may seem initially—are well documented by transcripts from Congressional hearings, the Central Intelligence Agency Reading Library, several US patents, declassified documents, official government websites, and other official government documents. The relevant information I uncovered has been hiding in plain sight among a clutter of other information and disinformation.

In this book, I am going to point out to you what to look for and where to look. Once you see what I point out, you might be surprised at what has been hiding in plain sight.

I wrote this book so it can be understood by people of different ages—from high school students who are concerned about their friends to grandparents who are concerned about their grandchildren who are too preoccupied with smartphones.

This manuscript was written for an eBook. This printed book was derived from the eBook. The eBook has many hyperlinks denoted by blue letters much like an Internet news story that allows you quickly access more information. However, with a printed book, you must manually enter the URL into an Internet browser. An important document, *Memories for Life* has been taken down from the Defense Advanced Research Projects Agency (DARPA). It might still be available at https://web.archive.org/web/20040331065003/http:/www.nesc.ac.uk/esi/events/Grand_Challenges/proposals/Memories.

pdf. This document was part of DARPA's LifeLog project. It explains various privacy and public policy problems LifeLog would face. This document also looks like a developmental road map for Facebook. Mr. Mark Zuckerberg had to testify to Congress about various privacy and public issues that are clearly explained in this 2003 document. LifeLog was canceled by the Pentagon the same day that Facebook was founded.

This book contains many grammatical errors, punctuation errors, and style issues that are inconsistent with the *Chicago Manual of Style*. These errors are contained within quotation marks, and they are exactly as they appear in the original sources. Many of the errors were from government documents and websites. (Are you surprised?) The editors wanted to clean up the mistakes. However, I opted to include the direct quotations exactly as they were—mistakes included. I have added [sic] in cases that I believed many people would notice the error. Alternatively, if the error was minor and "[sic]" would draw attention the subtle error, I opted not to add "[sic]."

It is correct to address Frank Olson with either *Mr.* or *Dr.* since he earned a PhD and can thus be addressed with the honorific *Dr.* Congressional transcripts record his name with the honorific *Mr.* Therefore, you will see both used in this book and sometimes on the same page. When I quoted the Congressional transcripts, I quoted exactly and used *Mr.* Elsewhere I chose to use *Dr.* as the most appropriate honorific to honor this individual who was willing to stand up for his convictions, even though it cost him his life.

I hope you enjoy reading this book as much as I have enjoyed writing it.

Acknowledgements

I want to thank many people. Without their help, this book would have been a failure. They helped me do what I could not do myself. They helped me see things that I could not see. They even provided me with very helpful innumerable comments on the structure, tone, and scope of this book. Foremost, Andy Aguirre provided the title for this book as well as gave many excellent suggestions to steer this book in the right direction. Likewise, the following people provided numerous excellent recommendations to improve the manuscript: Scott Long, LPC-Intern; Lawrence Brown; Philip Fortenberry; Mac Fudge, DVM; Phleet Greear; KD Jost; John Maas, DVM; Mike Ramirez; J. Street Hall; Herb White; and Bill Wustenberg, DVM. Many reviewers were enthusiastic and provided great feedback; however, they requested that I not list their names.[b] Some reviewers were noticeably silent. The silence spoke volumes. I interpreted the silence as a polite sign that the manuscript needed significant improvements. As a result, I did a substantial rewrite.

I want to thank Zoe Quinton—a superb literary consultant—for her insight and suggestions.

Most importantly, I want to thank those who gave me clues about what to look for and where to look. Without their help, the truth would have remained hidden in plain sight. They shall remain unnamed.

---

b   The most common reason they cited but did not want their names listed would be for possible pushback from the intelligence community.

Introduction

This book intertwines upon my previous books—*Google Glass Can Read Your Mind* (2014) and *Cunningly Smart Phones: Deceit, Manipulation, and Private Thoughts Revealed.* (2015).

Much has changed since I published my previous books. Then it seems like everyone was in love with the new tech toys and social media. Saying anything bad about Google, Google Glass, Facebook, or smartphone^c was like telling someone that their baby was ugly. Nevertheless, some are now beginning to question their relationship with their smartphones, hence the title of this book.

You should read this book if any of the following applies to you:

✓ You have ever felt the need to check your smartphone because of a sound or "just because."
✓ You know someone who is addicted to smartphone.
✓ You want to know what cocaine, amphetamines, sex, and sugar have in common with smartphones.

Who Should Not Read This Book?

If you are comfortable being a mental slave or being covertly and remotely controlled, do not waste your time reading this book. It may make you angry or even violent like the prisoners in Pluto's *Allegory*

---

c   The author uses the terms "smartphone" and "smartphones" to be inclusive of *smart* devices such as *smart* speakers, *smart* watches, wearable *smart* devices, *smart* TVs, *smart* homes, *smart* cities, personal digital assistants, *smart* doorbells, other *smart* devices, and Internet of Things (IoT) devices. They share several characteristics. They connect to the internet. They promise to make your experiences more enjoyable and pleasurable.

of the Cave. [d][4] Alternatively, if you want to see the sunshine and know and learn more about what is really going on in the world around you, brace yourself because smartphone obsession is just the tip of the proverbial iceberg. It will challenge some of your beliefs. It may even make you angry when you realize how your trust has been betrayed.

What Is in This Book?

From this book, you will learn what many on the other side of the veil of secrecy did not want you to know. That may sound like another tinfoil hat conspiracy theory; however, it is not. This book is very well documented by transcripts from Congressional hearings, various Central Intelligence Agency websites, US patents, declassified documents and other official government documents, scientific studies, and articles from reputable news organizations.

A Summary

- ✓ Smartphone addiction and cocaine addiction are both enabled by the same pleasure/reward pathway in the brain.

- ✓ A chemical in the brain (dopamine) plays a powerful role in the brain's pleasure/reward system.

- ✓ Dopamine is responsible for the emotional part of the pleasure/reward system.

- ✓ Pleasure from sex is registered in the brain by dopamine.

- ✓ Cocaine addiction is facilitated by dopamine.

- ✓ Parents often use smartphones as digital babysitters. Some parents are now concerned; however, those videos on smartphones are "disturbingly effective in enrapturing young children."[5]

- ✓ Tech companies and tech billionaires have become the high-tech equivalent of pimps, prostitutes, and drug dealers selling cocaine. They have figured out how to design smartphones and apps to release small squirts of dopamine in your brain.

---

d   For more information about the prisoners in Pluto's *Allegory of the Cave,* please read the footnote in the Preface section.

✓ Many former tech insiders now regret their efforts that helped the tech companies design smartphones and apps that cause the dopamine release in your brain and the resulting addiction.

✓ The Central Intelligence Agency (CIA) funded research on dopamine [6] as part of Project MKULTRA, [7] (pronounced M-K-ULTRA[8]). This was a mind-control and behavioral-modification program.

✓ Project MKULTRA might have remained hidden from public view forever. However, the CIA was concerned that one of their top scientists might blow the whistle on their programs.

✓ One of the CIA's top scientists died under mysterious circumstances. The CIA told his family he committed suicide.

Up to this point, this might seem like a spy novel with the CIA trying to control agents, cocaine, sex, and a top scientist dying under mysterious circumstances—it is not. Unfortunately, these are all true. However, only the CIA could have laid the foundation for this weird reality. Nevertheless, let us continue with the summary:

✓ The CIA covered up Dr. Frank Olson's death. However, after two decades, two Congressional hearings, [e] a presidential commission,[f] and a public apology by President Ford, the false narrative constructed by the CIA was shattered and the fact about Dr. Frank Olson's death finally came to light.

✓ The Olson family went public and sued the CIA. President Ford invited the Olson family to the White House and issued an official public apology for the death of Dr. Frank Olson.

---

e   The first Congressional hearing was in 1975—United States Senate Select Committee to Study Governmental Operations with Respect to Intelligence Activities, 1975 Note. This is also known as the Church Committee after Senator Frank Church whom served as the chairperson of the committee. The second Congressional hearing was in 1977—Project MKULTRA, The CIA'S Program of Research in Behavioral Modification, Joint Hearing Before The Select Committee On Intelligence And The Subcommittee On Health And Scientific Research Of The Committee On Human Resources United States Senate Ninety-Fifth Congress, First Session, August 3, 1977

f   United States President's Commission on CIA Activities within the United States. This is also called the Rockefeller Commission and was headed by Vice President Nelson Rockefeller.

The Olson family received $750,000 and dropped their lawsuit against the CIA.

✓ *Dr. Frank Olson did not die in vain.* Without his death and his family's audacity to call out the CIA, we probably would have never learned about Project MKULTRA [9] and the CIA's researches about dopamine, mind control, and behavior modification that became public knowledge because of A Joint Hearing Before The Select Committee On Intelligence And The Subcommittee On Health And Scientific Research Of The Committee On Human Resources United States Senate Ninety-Fifth Congress. [10]

✓ The Department of Defense (DoD) published an unclassified memorandum in 1977 that showed how the money for dopamine research flowed from the CIA through the US Navy to civilian universities, contractors, and other civilian organizations. [11]

✓ The intelligence community has funded many tech companies through a venture capital firm called In-Q-tel (IQT). [12] A CBS News article alleged to have established a connection between the CIA and Google, social media, and other tech companies. [13]

✓ The "tinfoil hat conspiracy theory" is debunked. Contrary to the common comedian parody, remote manipulation of the nervous system is a real phenomenon and is documented in several patents. You may be surprised what might happen if you do not use a tinfoil hat. You can read more about that in the chapter titled, "Electronic, Magnetic, and Acoustic Viagra."

✓ Many events and programs portrayed in the *Jason Bourne* movie series parallel various CIA MKULTRA [14] mind-control programs.

✓ Some allege that the CIA halted its mind-control program. However, closer examination of testimony to Congress reveals that the CIA only alleged to have stopped mind-control research that particularly involved drugs. Many mind-control and behavior-modification subprograms did not involve drugs. Did those other subprograms continue?

✓ *Covert* ~~brainwashing~~[15] "influencing" is the new reality. US Patent 8,095,492 references the CIA Project MKULTRA's [16] brainwashing techniques and artificial intelligence in its patented process that can *covertly*[g] "influence" people "towards a desired outcome." [17]

✓ It started as "brain warfare."[18] It started as a battle for the mind in a generic sense. As the technology improved, it changed to a battle for *your* mind.

✓ Tech companies and tech billionaires have amassed fortunes by using CIA mind-control research in ways it was never intended.

✓ The CIA mind-control and behavior-modification research was meant to *protect* us from spies, double agents, and our enemies.

✓ Instead, the CIA mind-control and behavior-modification research has been used by cunning people within our own country to *exploit* us.

✓ It is a large tangled web and who knows what are entangled in this web. Jeffrey Epstein has been exposed as a pedophile that allegedly used honey traps to compromise people.

✓ Allegedly, Jeffrey Epstein boasted, "I Collect People, I Own People, I Can Damage People."[19] Jeffrey Epstein alleged he had dirt on many prominent people in technology circles in Silicon Valley.[20]

✓ Mr. Acosta—President Trump's secretary of labor—suddenly resigned when it was revealed that he was associated with Jeffrey Epstein's unusually light plea bargain.

✓ Smartphone addiction may fuel the next wave of litigation as big as the tobacco and opioid litigation. Tech

---

g " 'Power produces influence' chart is made as to which forms of overt, **covert**, and bridging influence are available to be applied." US Patent 8,095,492.

companies knew that dopamine has facilitated addiction to smartphones just as it does for opioids and nicotine. Tech companies refused attempts to limit addiction. Dopamine has facilitated smartphone addiction, and this can lead to anxiety, depression, decreased patience, and physical problems. Many innocent people were already injured and killed by smartphone-addicted drivers distracted by their smartphones.

✓ Who will protect the little children from addition?

Will you win your own mind battle and preserve your freedom of thought? Will you lose? Are you willing to let someone hack your brain[21] [22] and remotely and covertly use "influencing strategies" and "influence actions" to "influence" you "towards" a "desired outcome" that you did not choose? The choice is yours. This book will show you what is really going on behind a veil of secrecy, so you have a better chance of winning if you do not want to be a mental slave. The final chapter includes suggestions that may help you win against those using "brain warfare"[23] in the battle to control *your* mind.[h]

Who Is the Intended Audience?

I wrote this book for high school students who are concerned about the damage smartphones are causing to our society. I also wrote this so that grandparents can understand why their grandchildren are too preoccupied with smartphones. Everyone else concerned about smartphones will benefit by reading this book.

---

[h]   Previously, brainwashing and brain warfare have been the preferred terms for secular discussion. The term *battle for the mind* is often associated with religious doctrine and sermons. In this book, I use terms "battle for your mind" without the religious connotation. The term *battle for your mind* is now more appropriate since the US Patent Office awarded patent 8,095,492 in 2012 that can covertly use "influencing strategies" to influence people toward a "desired outcome." This computer program can tailor an individual program for people. It can also track the progress and adjust the "influencing strategies" as need to achieve a covert "desired outcome." Therefore, the term *battle for your mind* more accurately reflects recent technological developments in a secular sense.

Is Your Smartphone Your Possession or Your Obsession?

"Is your smartphone your possession or your obsession?" — *Andy Aguirre*

Do you own your smartphone, or does it own you?

Smartphones Were Cleverly Designed to Be Your BFF

Smartphones and other smart devices[24] have become silicone-based Best Friends Forever (S-B BFFs). These connect people with their carbon-based Best Friends Forever (C-B BFFs). For many, smartphones and other smart devices have become the primary communication link to the world, replacing face-to-face communication. Smartphones can also serve as a barrier to protect people from a world that is often demanding and sometimes mean, hateful, ugly, and repulsive. Smartphones also give people power to control how much they want to interact with the world.

How did smartphone become so intertwined with people's lives? Here are just a few reasons.

The clever use of the word *smart* has a double meaning. The word *smart* indicates that phones are more capable than an old-fashioned cell phone. *Smart* implies that if you are not using a smartphone, you are using a dumb phone. Who wants to be associated with something dumb? Peer pressure has been used as a great marketing strategy.

Paradoxically, several studies show that smartphones may weaken the intellect instead of making some people smarter.[25] According to

1

an article in Scientific American, "when people call up information through their devices, they often end up suffering from delusions of intelligence. They feel as though "their *own* mental capacities" had generated the information, not their devices. "The advent of the 'information age' seems to have created a generation of people who feel they know more than ever before."[26]

Smartphone cameras delight many. By utilizing these cameras and by having the ease of sending photos, people can record joyful moments and instantly send them to friends or post their pictures on social media. Smartphones have therefore become a prerequisite for any joyful events.

Most smartphones use either Android (Google) or iOS (Apple) software platform. Both Apple and Google have encouraged thousands of third-party software developers to produce new apps for smartphones. These apps have simplified many daily tasks. These have been so successfully used by people, causing the escalation of difficulties for anyone to take part in the society, to communicate with family and friends, or to function in a job without a smartphone.

One survey showed that over one-half the people using smartphones fear losing it.[27] Over 70 percent of people keep their smartphone within five feet.[28] This data is over five years old. The numbers have probably skyrocketed in 2019.

One source offers several statistics:[29]

- ✓ 47% of parents think their children are addicted to their smartphones.
- ✓ 67% of surveyed teachers observed students being negatively distracted by mobile devices.
- ✓ 50% of parents are concerned for the impact smartphones on their children's mental health.
- ✓ 58% have tried to reduce usage but only 41% were successful.

This source contains many other useful statistics.

There are many wonderful smartphone technologies and great features. However, some of these features may covertly cause addiction and depression. Even though your smartphone may seem like your BFF, it may not truly be true at all. Anyone is susceptible to experience addiction and depression due to using this said device and its features. Smartphones do not often enrich someone's life as a carbon-based friend. Consider that brain scans show that "addicted teenagers had significantly higher scores in depression, anxiety, insomnia severity and impulsivity" as the result of using smartphones.[30] A recent study showed "use of Facebook was negatively associated with well-being."[31]

Is it possible that your smartphone was cleverly designed to be the electronic equivalent of drug dealers, electronic pimps, and electronic prostitutes? Were smartphones designed to get people hooked on dopamine—the same as street drug dealers get people hooked on cocaine? As known by many, having sex stimulates the brain to release dopamine. Pimps and prostitutes profit from stimulating the release of dopamine by selling sex.

"Dopamine has been identified as the critical neurotransmitter in the reward circuitry mediating substance abuse and the primary focus of preclinical research and clinical treatment interventions."[32] Drug addiction and smartphone addiction both use dopamine to active the pleasure reward circuitry in the brain.

Society treats one group like criminals for manipulating dopamine in the brain. Yet, the other group also manipulates dopamine, and they are treated like rock stars. Both groups manipulate dopamine in the brain. Why are the two groups treated differently?

Perhaps, some do not understand what dopamine is and how it functions in the brain.

The next chapter will examine how many were unwittingly sucked into this elaborate swindle based on dopamine. Then the following chapter will explain how dopamine emotionally excites the brain whether the stimulant is cocaine, amphetamine, sex, sugar, or smartphone.

I Want Dopamine, and I Want It Now!

Smartphone incorporates several technologies that cause the brain to release small squirts of dopamine into the pleasure reward pathways of the brain.[33] Regardless of whether the initial stimulation comes from drugs or activities, dopamine sends a pleasure signal to the brain.[34] People can become addicted to their smartphone the same way they can become addicted to cocaine.

How did we get into this mess? Partial answers are printed everywhere but no one else has been willing to answer that question completely. Perhaps others did not know where to look. Maybe they could not invest the effort to dig up the underlying facts. Maybe they were afraid to report what they found. Maybe other writers were under the spell of the Mighty Wurlitzer[35]—or some reincarnation of it. What better place to find a commentary of Hugh Wilford's book *The Mighty Wurlitzer: How the CIA Played America* than from the CIA reading library.

"Wilford explains the title derived from a 1950s quip by CIA operational chief Frank Wisner, who reportedly spoke of his directorate's complex of front organizations as a "mighty Wurlitzer"; a big theater organ "capable of playing any propaganda tune he desired."[36]

Unbeknownst to many, the CIA funded dopamine research. The CIA was concerned that Russia (also known as USSR during the Cold War) had found ways to control the mind. A document available at the CIA reading library shows that Defense Intelligence Agency was closely following Russian (USSR) research on brainwashing, controlling behavior, and dopamine.[37] [38] The CIA did not want to be surprised, so they started their own research into mind control and behavior modification.

Many people are talking about smartphone addiction, and some are writing about dopamine's role in smartphone addiction. However, no one else has been willing to write about how and why the CIA funded research about dopamine in relevance to smartphone addiction.

On April 9, 2017, *60 Minutes* (CBS News) featured Anderson Cooper in "*What is 'brain hacking?' Tech insiders on why you should care.*"[39] Later on June 11, 2017, *60 Minutes* (CBS News) featured again Anderson Cooper in "*Hooked on your phone?*"[40] Both of the *60 Minutes's* segments had linked smartphone addiction to dopamine.

Anderson Cooper completed an internship with the CIA.[41] Spurred on by my inkling that Anderson Cooper was only partially covering a hot topic while not exposing everything, I started digging. After much effort, I uncovered what Anderson Cooper did not mention in the two *60 Minutes's* segments on smartphone addiction and dopamine—the evidence that linked the CIA with dopamine. That proof was in the 1977 DoD memorandum that showed how the CIA used the DOD as a front and sent money through the DoD and to the US Navy that dispersed the money to universities and civilian researchers.[42] Several pages of this memo are included in the annex. The CIA funded dopamine research as part of Project MKULTRA,[43] which researched various methods of mind control and behavior modification. Project MKULTRA will be covered in a more detailed manner later in this book. To pique your interest, there are many parallels between the *Jason Bourne* movie series and the CIA's Project MKULTRA. Those parallels also will be covered later in this book.

In the *60 Minutes's* segment "*Hooked on your phone?*" former Google product manager, Tristan Harris stated, "They are shaping the thoughts and feelings and actions of people. They are programming people"[44] If you think Tristan's statement is just hyperbole, you should consider the title for CIA MKULTRA's subproject 141,[45] "*Program to obtain a feasible and practicable capability to influence and control human behavior.*" (Emphasis added.) Do you think there might be some similarities between the CIA's subproject 141 and what Tristan Harris alleges that Google is able to do? Dr. Robert Epstein testified to Congress that Google flipped least 2.6 million votes in the 2016 election.[46] You may think it is wonderful if Google can flip votes for the candidates you prefer. However, if Google flips votes for candidates you did not vote for, then you might believe that democracy could be subverted by technology. If you doubt that people can be programmed, you should read all of US Patent 8,095,492 that describes how computer programs can use "influencing strategies" to "influence" people "towards a desired outcome."[47]

These recent technological developments beg many questions. Has science fiction become reality? Have some unsuspecting people been sucked by an invisible electronic vortex into an altered state of mind similar to *The Matrix*?[i] [48] Should we offer those living in alternate reality the equivalent of a "red pill," or should we just leave them alone? What if we offer them a "red pill" and they become violent like the prisoners in Pluto's *Allegory of the Cave*?[j] What should we do about those who do not realize that their anxiety, depression, level of aggression, and patience threshold can be remotely controlled? Will suggesting that they are being remotely controlled only make them angrier since their patience threshold may already be low?

Smartphones are intentionally designed to make you anxious if you do not frequently[49] check them. Several studies have documented that smartphones increase anxiety.[50] [51] [52] Researcher Nancy Cheever states that current "research suggests our phones are keeping us in a continual state of anxiety in which the only antidote–is the phone."[53] The *New York Times* reports that tech companies understand the psychology of addiction and the addictive role of dopamine in the brain. They use this knowledge to "lace their products with "hijacking techniques" that lure us in and create "compulsion loops." [54] One study alleges the patience threshold is lower than ever before and technology is the reason.[55]

A private company in Venice California, Dopamine Labs,[56] specializes in writing algorithms that study millions of internet users.

---

i　　　　A science fiction movie about people unwitting living in a simulated reality with others are controlling their thought and existence.

j　　　　For more information about the prisoners in Pluto's *Allegory of the Cave,* please read the footnote in the Preface section.

Mr. Ramsay Brown and T. Dalton Combs, PhD—cofounders of Dopamine Labs—allege they have found an "addiction code." They allege they wrote software that tech companies use to keep you coming back for more dopamine.[57] To counter the addictive effect of dopamine, Mr. Brown and Dopamine Labs also produced an app called Space. This app helps reduce dopamine addiction by creating a twelve-second delay before it launches any social media app. Allegedly, Apple rejected it from their app store. According to Mr. Brown, Apple stated that "any app that would encourage people to use other apps or use their iPhone less was unacceptable for distribution in the apps store."[58]

I Am Terrified

Some former insiders who designed the dopamine traps now have regrets. A few are willing to talk publicly about their regrets. Roger McNamee is now the managing director and cofounder of Elevation Partners, an investment partnership focused on media/entertainment content and consumer technology. This is his comment regarding his involvement with Facebook:

> I was an early adviser to Facebook's team, but I am terrified by the damage being done by these Internet monopolies…the big Internet companies know more about you than you know about yourself, which gives them huge power to influence you, to persuade you to do things that serve their economic interests.[59]

Later in the book, we will look at patented processes[k] that can use information obtained about people to covertly ~~brainwash~~ "influence" people "towards a desired outcome." [60]

Roger McNamee interviewed ex-Facebook president Sean Parker. Parker regrets the damage being inflicted on children. Parker admits Facebook deliberately tried to addict users.[61] Parker also stated that Facebook has knowingly exploited a human vulnerability. "It's a social-validation feedback loop…exactly the kind of thing that a hacker like myself would come up with, because you're exploiting a vulnerability in human psychology."[62] Continuing on, he stated, "The same can be

---

k   US Patent 8,095,492

said about tobacco companies and drug dealers."[63] (We will compare the similarities of dopamine to tobacco in another chapter "Are Other Legal Remedies Available?")

Sean Parker went on and "explained that when Facebook was being developed the objective was: "How do we consume as much of your time and conscious attention as possible?" It was this mindset that led to the creation of features such as the "like" button that would give users "a little dopamine hit" to encourage them to upload more content."[64]

Another insider was Chamath Palihapitiya, the vice president for user growth at Facebook until 2011. Years after leaving Facebook, he admitted that he felt "tremendous guilt" about what he did for Facebook, and he stated,[65]

> The short-term, dopamine-driven feedback loops that we have created are destroying how society works. No civil discourse, no cooperation, misinformation, mistruth… This is not about Russian ads… This is a global problem. It is eroding the core foundations of how people behave by and between each other.

There were other former insiders who also voiced out their regrets. Justin Rosenstein was the creator of Facebook's "Like" button that was "wildly" successful. User "engagement soared as people enjoyed the short-term boost they got from giving or receiving social affirmation, while Facebook harvested valuable data about the preferences of users that could be sold to advertisers. It was so successful that Twitter, Instagram and many other platforms used the same idea." Rosenstein also offers that, "It is revealing that many of these younger technologists are weaning themselves off their own products, sending their children to elite Silicon Valley schools where iPhones, iPads and even laptops are banned."[66]

Tristan Harris was a Google employee. He is now a critic of the tech industry. As a former insider, his insights are poignant, "Our choices are not as free as we think they are." [67] Compare that comment to information found in US Patent 8,095,492 *Method and system for providing and analyzing influence strategies.* This patent cites brainwashing research conducted by the CIA's Project MKULTRA.[l] The patent alleges that a computer program can "influence" people "towards a desired outcome."[68] It also contains the words "artificial intelligence."

Chris Marcellino is a co-inventor of Apple's patent for "managing notification connections and displaying icon badges" (US Patent 8,135,392). He also has regrets.

> Honestly, at no point was I sitting there thinking: let's hook people... All of it is reward-based behaviour that activates the brain's dopamine pathways." Although he was once an insider and profited from his work, he "is conflicted about the ethics of exploiting people's psychological vulnerabilities.

The Royal Society for Public Health stated the following:[69] [m]

- ✓ Rates of anxiety and depression in young people have risen to 70 percent in the past twenty-five years.
- ✓ Social media use is linked with increased rates of anxiety, depression and poor sleep.
- ✓ Social media has been described as more addictive than cigarettes and alcohol.

In another chapter in this book, we will dig deeper into these issues. First, let us look closer at how dopamine can cause addiction.

---

[l] The CIA's Project MKULTRA will be explored in more detail in a later chapter.

[m] Based on 1,479 people aged fourteen to twenty-four years.

Dopamine—Dependence, Addiction, and Tolerance

D opamine is a chemical produced in the brain that affects specific parts of the brain. It is central to understanding how people become addicted. Dopamine is involved with the reward pathways in the brain.[70] Dopamine also "plays a critical role in the processing of addictive qualities of drugs." [71] There are many parts of the brain involved with the reward pleasure pathways, but dopamine is released during emotional processing.[72] [73] It provides the brain with the perception of "Wow!" Some people want more wow experiences and can become addicted to the dopamine release in their brain. The wow experience from dopamine can occur as the result of *drugs* (such as cocaine,[74] amphetamines,[75] etc.) or *activities* (such as using smartphones,[76] having sex,[77] watching pornography,[78] video gaming,[79] gambling,[80] etc.).

Dopamine is not always bad. Dopamine has many positive effects.[81] In fact, most of the time, it helps steer us in the right direction. For example, exercise is healthy, and it can increase dopamine activity in our brain.[82] Although dopamine normally serves an obliging role, unscrupulous tech companies and tech billionaires have figured out how to hijack people's brain by covertly manipulating it.

Consider the absurdity of the current laws, regulations, and business ethics. If a drug dealer sells an illegal drug that stimulates the release of dopamine, they can be arrested and thrown in jail, and their assets seized. If tech companies or tech billionaires use your smartphone to stimulate the release of dopamine in your brain, it is perfectly legal. Furthermore, they are considered geniuses and are praised by investors for delivering windfall profits. If dopamine is administered intravenously as a drug, the Food and Drug Administration must approve it. Dopamine must have a packet insert that clearly explains how the drug works, indications, side effects, warning, etc.[83] However, if someone covertly uses your smartphone to hack your brain and manipulates it with dopamine, there are no regulations, no approval processes, and no warnings.

Many people oppose new regulations. Nevertheless, covertly hacking the brain and dopamine manipulation may warrant new regulations. The current situation is reminiscent of the Wild West, where morphine and heroin were unregulated and crooks amassed vast fortunes by using those drugs to manipulate dopamine in the brain. Some use cocaine, amphetamine, morphine, heroin, etc. to stimulate the brain with dopamine, while others use smartphones.

"What is past is prologue." This phrase is attributed to William Shakespeare and is engraved on a statue on the northeast corner of the National Archives Building in Washington, DC. Morphine was widely used in the Civil War to relieve pain from battle wounds. After the Civil War, addiction increased in the civilian population. However, physicians took the lead in educating themselves and the public about the dangers of addiction and the problem decreased in most of the United States.[84]

Smartphones are addictive just like morphine, which is a derivative of opium. Indeed, "What is past is prologue." Both addictions use dopamine to stimulate the brain's pleasure/reward center. In 2016, American Academy of Pediatrics "released a new policy statement to help families create and foster a healthy 'media diet' for their kids."[85] Robert Lustig, MD has written a book to educate the public about problems caused by smartphones, *The Hacking of the American Mind: The Science Behind the Corporate Takeover of Our Bodies and Brains* (2017). I applaud these efforts, and I encourage other health care providers to take the challenge to educate the public about the hazards of smartphone addiction, as physicians a century ago were able to warn and alert the public about the dangers of morphine and opium.

The Almonds

Many structures in the brain are associated with the pleasure/reward system.[86] Unfortunately, they all are named in Latin. Many find those Latin terms difficult to pronounce or remember. You can learn them if you wish. However, knowing their Latin names may not help you understand how dopamine facilitates addiction.

Fortunately, the main structure in the brain associated with dopamine translates into English as a word that describes its shape. In the rest of this book, we will not use the Latin name *amygdala*. Instead, we will use the English translation—*almond*—because that is how it is shaped.

Since there are two almonds—one on each side of the brain—we often refer them in the plural "almonds." Urban slang is rife with the terms such as *stimulates my almonds, tickles my almonds,* and *activates my almonds.* These phrases mean that someone's pleasure/reward pathway in the brain has been stimulated with dopamine. Many other parts of the brain are associated with the pleasure response. However, the almonds (amygdala) are the parts of the brain that are primarily responsible for the emotional part of the said experience.[87] As a result, dopamine is associated with dependency on opiates, cannabis, nicotine, amphetamine, methamphetamine, and cocaine.[88] The emotional stimulation dopamine provides could be from an activity, a drug, or something as common as eating sugar and getting a sugar high.[89]

The previous explanations are just summaries. If you want to learn more, I recommend reading *The Hacking of the American Mind: The Science Behind the Corporate Takeover of Our Bodies and Brains* (2017). The best-selling author, Robert Lusting, MD, explains how dopamine, which is chemical, interacts with the nerves in the brain so that endogenous opioid-like chemicals are released creating much the same effect as morphine or heroin.[90] As Dr. Lusting explains, "Virtually all pleasurable activities (sex, alcohol, food, gambling, shopping, and the internet) employ the dopamine pathway in the brain to generate the motivation."[91]

Smartphone and video game addiction is obvious in our society. We can see and observe it all around us. We all have seen people that impulsively interact with their smartphones rather than the world as well as the people around them. Smartphone addiction results from dopamine addiction. Some people are more vulnerable to dopamine addiction than others.[n] [92] Similarly, some people appear to be easily addicted to smartphone while others are not so much. There are genetic variations regarding people's susceptibility to dopamine-mediated dependency and addiction. Current research shows that addictions "are moderately to highly heritable."[93] Tolerance is also heritable.[94] This suggests that genetic variation may explain why some people are easily addicted, while others are more resistant to smartphone addiction. One source alleges, "40% of the population is addicted to their smartphones," and "1 in 3 mobile owners would rather give up sex than their phones."[95]

Although the World Health Organization (WHO) has not called out smartphones, it has already called out video gaming that also utilizes dopamine. In September 2018, the WHO included gaming disorder in the 11th Revision of the International Classification of Diseases (ICD-11) as the following:

> [A] pattern of gaming behavior ("digital-gaming" or "video-gaming") characterized by impaired control over gaming, increasing priority given to gaming over other activities to the extent that gaming takes precedence over other interests and daily activities, and continuation or escalation of gaming despite the occurrence of negative consequences... For gaming disorder to be diagnosed, the behavior pattern must be of sufficient severity to result in significant impairment in personal, family, social, educational, occupational, or other important areas of functioning and would normally have been evident for at least 12 months.[96]

Drug abuse, smartphone, and video game addiction are similar in that they all use dopamine and the same neuron pathways in the brain. National Institute of Drug Abuse (NIDA) has many webpages that explain dopamine and addiction in more detail. My explanation below is just a summary. Please go to their webpages if you want a more detailed explanation with both text and graphics.

---

n   "Understanding why some individuals are more vulnerable to becoming addicted to drugs than others remains one of the most challenging questions in drug abuse research."

In the discussion below, we need to establish and signify some orientations regarding what direction the nerve impulse travels. We can trace the electrical transmission from one nerve cell (neuron) to the next nerve cell (neuron). Water flows down in rivers and streams. Likewise, an electrical signal travels from the upstream neuron to the downstream neuron. In a nutshell, neurons can be called upstream neurons[o] and downstream neurons indicating which direction an electrical signal travels. There is one problem, however. The electrical impulse does not flow continuously like water in a river.

There is a small gap between neurons called the synaptic gap or synapse. In a more technical description, neurons are classified as presynaptic neurons (upstream neurons) or postsynaptic neurons (downstream neurons). An electrical impulse travels down the presynaptic neuron. At the end of the presynaptic neuron, the electrical impulse results in the release of chemicals (neurotransmitters) into the synaptic gap that bind to receptors on the postsynaptic neuron. The binding of neurotransmitters to receptors results in a newly generated electrical impulse traveling down the postsynaptic neuron. Modern fiber optic cables need optical repeaters to regenerate optical signals since these degrade with distance. A synapse is like a repeater. Synapses can also modulate nerve impulses in cases of addiction, especially in cases of down regulation that leads to tolerance.

---

[o]   This is a simplification to facilitate understanding. The nervous system is divided into two parts—the peripheral nervous system and the central nervous system (the brain and spinal cord). In the peripheral nervous system, *efferent* nerve fibers *exit* a particular region. They carry an electrical impulse away from a particular region. For example, efferent nerves carry the electrical impulse from the spinal cord to muscles. *Afferent* nerve fibers *arrive* at a particular place in the spinal cord or brain. For example, afferent nerves carry an electrical impulse from sensory neurons in the skin to the spinal cord. From the spinal cord, the electrical impulse travels up another afferent neuron to the brain. The brain then senses hot, cold, pressure, etc. Thing get a more complicated in the brain as billions of neurons are coursing through the brain. One neuron may have many fibers that relay electrical impulses to many other neurons. However, as a rule in a given brain region, afferents are arriving fibers while efferents are exiting fibers.

In the brain,[p] dopamine is released from the end of the presynaptic neuron into the synaptic gap. The dopamine in the synaptic gap binds to receptors on the postsynaptic neuron and initiates another electrical impulse that travels down the neuron to the next synaptic gap and then next neuron and so on.

Dopamine binds receptors on postsynaptic neuron for a very short time. The dopamine is quickly released back into the synaptic gap, and the presynaptic neuron pumps the dopamine back into small vacuoles where it is ready to be released again.

The mechanism of addiction graphics from National Institute of Drug Abuse (NIDA) that may increase your understanding. Although they focus on drug abuse, the mechanism of addiction is almost the same[q] whether it is from addictive drugs or smartphones.

- An electrical impulse travels down a nerve cell (neuron) until it reaches the end of the neuron.
- The electrical impulse causes the neuron to release dopamine from tiny vacuoles near the membrane at the end of the upstream neuron.
- The dopamine crosses the space between the two neurons— the synaptic gap. The dopamine in synaptic gap binds to special dopamine receptors on the downstream neuron.
- This causes an electrical impulse to travel along the length of the downstream neuron.
- After a short time interval, the downstream neuron releases dopamine from its receptors and the dopamine floats back into the synaptic gap.
- From the synaptic gap, upstream neuron pumps dopamine back into the vacuoles at the end of the neuron.

---

p   Some—but not all—neurons in the brain release dopamine into the synaptic gap. Other neurotransmitter used by neurons in the brain include serotonin and acetylcholine. There is a long list of neurotransmitters. The purpose of this footnote is not to cover all neurotransmitters but rather to show that dopamine is not the only neurotransmitter.

q   The process of stimulating the release of dopamine that in turn stimulates the almonds (amygdala) is simpler for smartphones addiction than addiction by drugs. In cases of drug addiction, more receptors and intermediate chemical messengers may be required to stimulate the release of dopamine that in turn stimulates the almonds (amygdala).

In summary, dopamine is released from presynaptic neurons (upstream neurons) to activate receptors on the postsynaptic neurons (downstream neurons), and then it is pumped back into the presynaptic neurons (upstream neurons). This is the so-called dopamine loop.

Another concept necessary to understand is *tolerance*.

> Tolerance happens when a person no longer responds to a drug in the way they did at first. So it takes a higher dose of the drug to achieve the same effect as when the person first used it. This is why people with substance use disorders use more and more of a [sic] drug to get the "high" they seek.[97]

The brain protects itself from overstimulation as a survival mechanism. The brain and the body cannot "red line" for long without causing serious harm or death. The brain protects itself by downregulation in which the brain decreases the number of receptors that recognize dopamine and therefore more dopamine is required to get the same effect.[r][98] These mechanisms facilitate tolerance and addiction.[99]

The four diagrams on the following pages may help those that learn better from visual images. These graphics are a simplified view of how dopamine works.[s] These diagrams are figurative and not literal.

---

r   This reference cites heroin. Downregulation works in a similar manner for both dopamine and heroin. Many times in this book, I cite examples related to cocaine, heroin, amphetamine, etc. because there is much more literature on drug addiction than dopamine addiction even though the final pathway in the brain is dopamine activating the pleasure/reward pathway in the brain.

s   Rather than drawing different diagrams for every possible permutation—and there are many—I opted to only draw four diagrams and use dopamine as a representation for dopamine and any drug that can directly activate the pleasure/reward system like dopamine. Drugs that mimic the effect of dopamine are called dopaminergic agents.

The process is more complicated, so a simplified explanation is a good place to start. Moreover, there are other chemicals and other parts of the brain involved in these complex processes. If you want to know more about the entire process, more details are provided in the footnotes.[t][u]

---

t   There are more parts of the brain involved with the reward/pleasure pathway than just the amygdala (almond). They include the ventral tegmental area (VTA) in the midbrain, amygdala, nucleus accumbens, cingulate gyrus, hippocampus, olfactory bulb, and medial prefrontal cortex.

The amygdala, nucleus accumbens, and hippocampus are part of the mesolimbic system.

Ventral tegmental area dopamine neurons are the primary source of dopamine in other structures in the pleasure/reward pathway.

Opioids, cocaine, amphetamine, and some other drugs directly affect dopamine receptors. They directly activate dopamine receptors in the pleasure/reward center without having to activate neurons to release dopamine on their behalf that in turn activates dopamine receptors in the pleasure/reward center. Other drugs such as nicotine bind to acetylcholine receptors that indirectly cause dopamine release within the reward system. https://www.ncbi.nlm.nih.gov/pmc/articles/PMC3036556/

https://www.ncbi.nlm.nih.gov/pubmed/18316420

Dopamine's effect on the downstream neuron is modified by drugs like morphine. Morphine acts on four opioid receptors, mu, delta, kappa, and ORL1. Mu is the most important for this discussion. Morphine activation of mu receptors is different for neurons that transmit along the pleasure/reward pathways than for neuron involved in transmitting pain signals. For neurons that transmit along the pleasure/reward pathways, morphine causes release of dopamine and stimulation of pleasure/reward pathway.

For neurons that transmit pain signals, activation of mu receptor by morphine *decreases* the magnitude of the electrical pulse on the downstream neuron, thus decreasing the sensation of pain.

More information can be found at the following links:

https://www.ncbi.nlm.nih.gov/pmc/articles/PMC3698859/

https://www.nature.com/articles/s41598-018-29915-4

https://www.sciencedaily.com/releases/2007/10/071014163647.htm

https://www.pbs.org/newshour/science/brain-gets-hooked-opioids

https://www.youtube.com/watch?v=YzCYuKX6zp8

https://www.nejm.org/doi/full/10.1056/NEJMra1507771

https://www.ncbi.nlm.nih.gov/pmc/articles/PMC2851054/

https://www.ncbi.nlm.nih.gov/pmc/articles/PMC2894302/

u   Dopamine and drugs that act like dopamine are portrayed in the diagrams as the center point for activating the pleasure/reward pathway. Some drugs can directly activate the pleasure/reward system, and other drugs need to use dopamine as an intermediary to activate the pleasure reward system. In reality, opioids and other drugs can directly active the pleasure/reward pathway without using dopamine as an intermediary.

Diagram 1. Initial Experience - WOW!

© Jack Wedam 2019

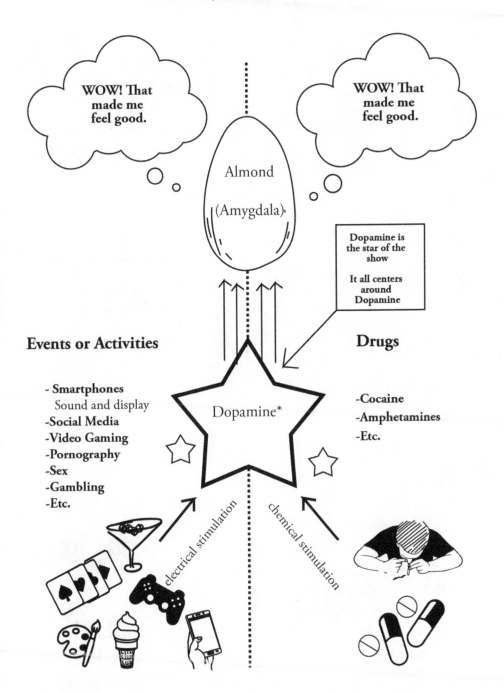

" Dopamine* activates the pleasure/reward system. Some drugs that act like dopamine can activate the pleasure/reward pathway directly without using dopamine as an intermediary."

Diagram 2. Dependency - I want more !

© Jack Wedam 2019

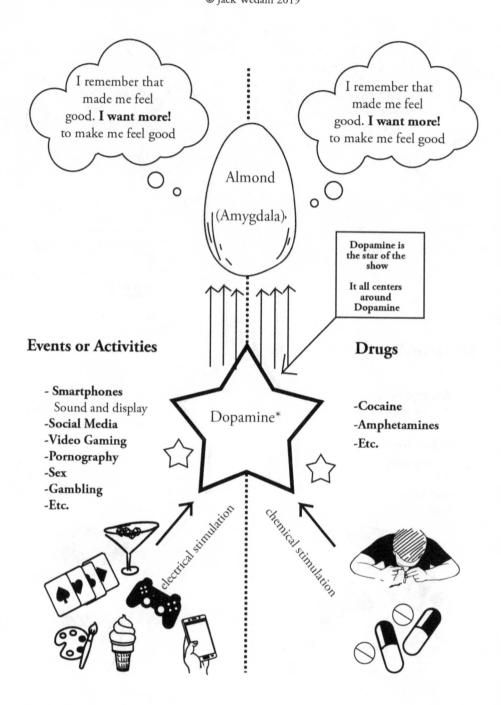

" Dopamine* activates the pleasure/reward system. Some drugs that act like dopamine can activate the pleasure/reward pathway directly without using dopamine as an intermediary."

Diagram 3. Tolerance
© Jack Wedam 2019

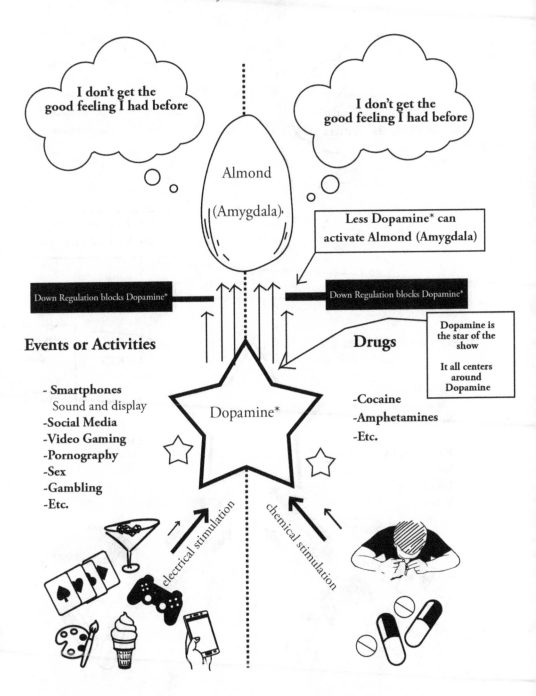

" Dopamine* activates the pleasure/reward system. Some drugs that act like dopamine can activate the pleasure/reward pathway directly without using dopamine as an intermediary."

Diagram 4. Addiction
© Jack Wedam 2019

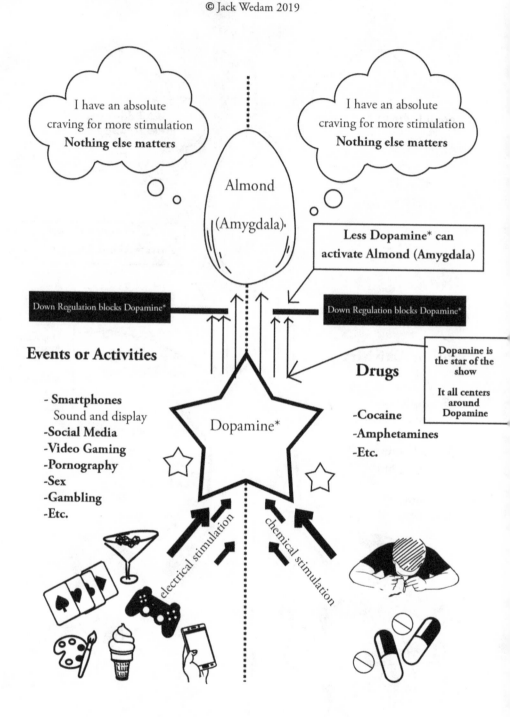

" Dopamine* activates the pleasure/reward system. Some drugs that act like dopamine can activate the pleasure/reward pathway directly without using dopamine as an intermediary."

The term smartphone addiction is now commonly used. Perhaps, at this point, we should inject some clarity. Opioid addiction is a national problem affecting many.

In 2017, more than 47,000 Americans died as a result of an opioid overdose, including prescription opioid, heroin, and illicitly manufactured fentanyl, a powerful synthetic opioid. That same year, an estimated 1.7 million people in the United States suffered from substance use disorders related to prescription opioid pain relievers.[100]

Like dopamine, some opioids can activate receptors in the pleasure/reward pathways. Stimulation of the pleasure/reward pathway is essentially the same regardless of whether the stimulation is initiated by cocaine, opioid, smartphone, or video gaming. Since opioids affect the brain in a similar manner as dopamine, discussion of dependence and addiction are relevant to both.

There are some subtle differences; however, the activation of the pleasure/reward pathway in the brain is similar for cocaine and opioid. The differences are which of the several dopamine receptors are activated. Cocaine and opioid activate D3 receptors. (Dopamine is a major neurotransmitter in the central nervous system, and among other functions is directly related to the rewarding effects of drugs of abuse. Dopamine signaling is mediated by D1, D2, D3, D4, and D5 receptors. The dopamine D3 receptor is a known target to treat a variety of neuropsychiatric disorders, including substance use disorders [e.g. cocaine and opioid], schizophrenia, and depression.)

Some clinicians and psychologists do not use a singular definition of drug addiction disorder. Instead, they often define two disorders—dependence and addiction.[101] The difference between the two depends mostly on the severity of the symptoms. Severity of symptoms increases along a continuum instead of stepwise. In the case of opioids, dependence versus addiction is defined by factors such as withdrawal symptoms, intensity of cravings, and how much risk people are willing to take just to satisfy their cravings.

I could find no clear definition of dependency versus addiction in the case of smartphones. Be that as it may, I propose that any of the following symptoms would indicate smartphone dependency:

- Resistance in giving up a smartphone for more than three hours
- Irritation or agitation if a smartphone is misplaced or missing for more than five minutes
- Irritation or agitation if someone takes a smartphone away
- Preference to interact with smartphone instead of people in near proximity

Furthermore, I propose that any of the following symptoms would indicate smartphone addiction:

- Any interaction with smartphones while driving such as gaming, texting, and visually monitoring social media (Excluded from this definition would be making phone calls under conditions such as hands-free talking that may be legal in your location.)
- Lack of awareness of people, animals, or moving objects in near proximity while interacting with a smartphone
- Continued interaction with a smartphone even if it means delaying for more than thirty minutes the normal bodily necessities such as eating if hungry, drinking to relieve thirst, or going to the restroom
- Holds on to a smartphone like Scrat holds on to an acorn in the *Ice Age*[102] movie series.

On a more serious note, the above classifications—dependency and addiction—and their associated symptoms are not meant to be immutable and chiseled into stone. Rather, consider them as a starting point in a dialog. I offer them in an attempt to prod the scientific community to develop better-defined symptoms with fact-based science such as brain scans and other brain imaging tools. There is an online quiz.[103] However, it is based on self-reporting, it is limited in scope,[v] and it may be subjective. If we use the proposed definitions above, what many refer to as smartphone addiction will instead be smartphone

---

[v]   It only assesses four dimensions—"four dimensions of nomophobia: not being able to communicate, losing connectedness, not being able to access information, and giving up convenience."

dependency. I think we should redefine the term smartphone addiction so it parallels that of cocaine or heroin addiction. Otherwise, with too much hyperbole, some may become dismissive of both smartphone dependency and smartphone addiction.

There is excellent scientific data available for substance abuse.[104] Unfortunately, the current data for smartphone addiction is not as reliable for many reasons. Some propose that the "official name for smartphone addiction is *Nomophobia* which is defined as having a fear of not being with your phone."[105] However, that definition is flawed. Decades ago before smartphones, some people panicked if the copper wire landlines—that were their only option for communication— would go down. People decades ago were fearful if they would not have the means to call a fire department, an ambulance, or the police in cases of emergencies. The term *nomophobia* is a step in the right direction for raising awareness of smartphone addiction; however, it is not the same as addiction that results from dopamine. We need better data and better definitions of behaviors that indicate smartphone addiction.

Many people in this present era have been dependent on smartphones for making emergency calls, checking weather updates, searching traffic reports, etc. and other functions that do not elicit a dopamine response. Various people also depend on a smartphone to hail a ride from a ride service such as Uber™ or Lyft™, while others depend on smartphones for maps and directions in ways. Nonetheless, these activities have nothing to do with dopamine in stimulating the pleasure/reward pathway in the brain. Therefore, many would easily misunderstand if you said someone was suffering from smartphone dependency. A term such as smartphone-dopamine-opioid-like-chemically-induced dependency would be more correct, but it would be a very long awkward alphabetical procession.[w]

Perhaps we can use terms that easily denote whether the dopamine problem results in dependency or addiction. Therefore, I propose the following terms:

- Smartphone Associated Dopamine Dependency (SAD-D)
- Smartphone Associated Dopamine Addiction (SAD-A)

---

w   A rhetorical device attributed to Mark Twain in "The Awful German Language."

Yes, the SAD acronym is intentional.[x] If you become dependent or addicted to smartphones, it is more difficult to be happy. Small dopamine squirts may stimulate short burst of pleasure, but that does not equate to joy or happiness. In fact, the result often is just the opposite because chronic excessive reward eventually leads to both addiction and depression—the two most unhappy states of the human condition.[106]

How you ever seen someone become aggressive if their smartphone is taken away? High dopamine levels or low serotonin levels—resulting from spending too much time on smartphones—might be the cause. More than just aggression, serotonin is a neurotransmitter that mediated satisfaction, happiness and optimism. Serotonin levels are reduced in depression.[107] Over stimulation of dopamine depresses levels of another neurotransmitter—serotonin—that helps regulate emotions and behavior. Serotonin also inhibits aggression.[108] One study suggests there is an "inverse association between serotonin and dopamine levels during aggression...aggressive behavior is closely associated with increased dopamine activity."[109] Another study alleges the patience threshold is lower than ever before and technology is the reason.[110] This study suggests that technology alters dopamine-serotonin balance that results in decreased patience.[111] Do you think that some people, particularly drivers, have become more aggressive since smartphones have become more widely and publicly used?

Do you know anyone who is addicted to their smartphone and at the same time depressed? Depression is not caused by a single factor. Instead, depression is the result of a constellation of factors; however, overstimulation of dopamine and subsequent reduction of serotonin may be a contributive factor to depression.

Smartphones are alluring and seductive. These handy devices may provide a mirage of happiness; however, these often contribute depression. The result is a sad condition. Perhaps, that should be restated as a SAD—Smartphone Associated Depression—condition. To add insult to injury, those suffering from depression are forced to

---

x   If you want to include video gaming into the definitions, perhaps these would work:
- Electronic Device Associated Dopamine Dependency (EDAD-D)
- Electronic Device Associated Dopamine Addiction (EDAD-A)

pay for their own depression since they have to pay for their smartphone and the continuous internet connection.

The prevalence of major episodes of depression is highest for 18 to 25-year-olds and decreases with age.[y] [112] Smartphone ownership is highest in eighteen to twenty-nine-year-olds and decreases with age.[z] [113] Monthly use of smartphone apps was highest for eighteen to twenty-four-year-olds and decreases with age.[aa] [114]

I could not find any studies that examined correlations of depression and smartphone use for those younger than 18. Do you think there may be a correlation between those that are prone to depression and those that are more likely to be addicted? This might be a great research project for a sharp scientist or researcher to dig into. Have you noticed any signs and symptoms of depression among your friends or family members who spend a lot of time on their smartphones? Maybe smartphones have contributed a weighty influence to the constellation of factors that result in their depression.

That is enough dopamine for now. Next, let us look at how we got into this mess (spoiler alert—the usual suspects).

Then we will look at how some use dopamine and other mind-control methods and covertly remotely control the behaviors and desires of unsuspecting people.

---

y   Data for 2017 show rates of major episodes of depression as 13.1% for age 18–26, 7.7% for age 26–49, and 4.7% for ages 50 and older.

z   Data for 2017 of smartphone ownership as 94% for age 18–29, 89% for age 30–49, 73% for age 50–64, and 46% for ages 65 and older.

aa   Data for June 2016 shows 93.5 hours per month for age 18–24, 85.6 for age 25–34, 78.8 hours for age 35–44, 62.7 hours for age 45–54, 55.6 hours for ages 55–64, and 42.1 for ages 65 and older.

The Protagonist Did Not Die in Vain

This is a nonfiction book. It is filled with a vast amount of facts from a wide variety of sources. Nevertheless, the facts could be arranged along the plot lines common to novels. If we are to do so, here is how the plot lines may possibly be constructed.

The protagonist was a top scientist working for the CIA. He saw things that bothered him. He voiced his objections, and he soon thereafter died under mysterious circumstances. Without the cascade of events set off by the death of the protagonist, we probably would have never been able to see behind the veil of secrecy and uncover the connection between the CIA and dopamine. Furthermore, we would not have been able to see some facts about the various CIA mind-control systems and behavior-modification programs.

The antagonists were the CIA and their proxies that killed the protagonist because they were concerned that he might be a security risk. The CIA used the Mighty Wurlitzer to create false narratives to cover up the death of the protagonist and to continue their nefarious activities.

The rest of us are caught in the middle of an epic struggle set in motion decades ago between the protagonist and the antagonists. Maybe some among us may have already been sucked into an invisible electronic vortex that results in an altered state of mind facilitated by mind-control and behavior-modification technologies sponsored by the CIA. A reincarnation of the Mighty Wurlitzer may still be spinning false narratives.

Some may dismiss the description above as merely as a fanciful tale or just another conspiracy theory. However, if you continue reading, you can determine for yourself if there is any merit to the assertions mentioned above. You can interpret the facts and decide for yourself what happened and what may still be happening behind the veil of secrecy. You can decide for yourself if the CIA is still in control of the mind-control and behavior-modification technologies or if others now control those technologies.

You now have a choice between a red pill and a blue pill. What will you choose?

The Battle for Your Mind[ab]

The backstory of how we got into the mess of smartphone addiction is a very large tangled web that goes back a long way and involves numerous people. Understanding the backstory may help you understand and sort some things that may appear to be disconnected but are connected by the tangled web. This is a classic situation in which if you only look at a few individual trees, you can easily miss not only the enormity of the entire forest but also the clever ways predators use to capture their prey and the clever ways the prey use to avoid being the next meal of the predators. By understanding the backstory, you will be able to see through the false, cleverly designed narratives the way people are distracted and diverted away from facts. If you want to avoid being caught in the large tangled web, the rest of this book may be of interest to you.

Could something from the Forgotten War[115] [116] have large consequences today? In the case of dopamine, what happened several decades ago led to the current mess we are now facing.

---

ab   Previously *brainwashing* and *brain warfare* have been the preferred terms for secular discussion. The terms *battle for the mind* is often associated with religious doctrine and sermons. In this book, I use terms *battle for your mind* without the religious connotation. The terms *battle for your mind* is now more appropriate since the US Patent Office awarded patent 8,095,492 in 2012 that can covertly use "influencing strategies" to influence people toward a "desired outcome." This computer program can tailor an individual program for people. It can also track the progress and adjust the "influencing strategies" as needed to achieve a covert "desired outcome." Therefore, the terms *battle for your mind* more accurately reflects recent technological developments in a secular sense.

On June 25, 1950, North Korea was a client state of Russia[ac] and launched a surprise attack on its neighboring country, South Korea. This event was just one of the more series of embarrassing intelligence failures for the newly formed Central Intelligence Agency (CIA), which was established barely three years earlier in 1947. In 1948, just six months after it was established, the CIA failed to predict an uprising in Bogota, Columbia. Two days of bloody riots disrupted the Ninth Inter-American Conference and greatly embarrassed the Secretary of State George C. Marshall.[117] The CIA also failed to warn of the first Soviet atomic test. These are just a few of the several notable failures by the fledging CIA.[118]

The CIA intelligence reports showed a buildup of North Korean forces. However, the CIA did not provide President Truman "information to give any clue as to whether an attack was certain or when it was likely to occur."[119] According to the National Public Radio, South Korea and the United States were blindsided.[120] That is a true and factual statement. In this case, however, *blindsided* is a politically correct way of saying that it was a massive intelligence failure. The CIA's failure cost South Korea and the United States much blood and treasure. It was a failure that has shaped the CIA for decades. Furthermore, the second-order effects have largely affected the rest of the world in a very profound way.

There are numerous explanations as to why the US was blindsided. The Central Intelligence Agency like its predecessor—the Office of Strategic Services (OSS)—was focused on Eastern Europe.[121] [122] In particular, the CIA suspected that Germany and Communist Russia had perfected the mind-control and behavior-modification techniques. The CIA was afraid the Russians and Chinese might have a new secret weapon that was more effective than an atomic bomb for achieving military victory. [123]

After World War II, allied forces uncovered evidence in which German scientists experimented with drugs and hypnosis for

---

ac   In this book, *Russia* will be used, as it is known today instead of Union of Soviet Socialist Republics (USSR) as it was known then. The USSR disintegrated in 1991, and most of the land mass reverted to the old name Russia. Some of the former Soviet states on the periphery of historical Russia changed their names back to their historical names. For example, Ukraine.

interrogation.[124] The CIA was also concerned about the German rocket and airplane technology.[125] The CIA was trying to get as many German scientists as possible (and their scientific research papers) out of Germany and into the United States[126] before the Russians could find them. Many German scientists were secretly brought into the United States under *Operation Paperclip*. The CIA spent vast resources on *Operation Paperclip* and that was their main focus. North Korea and South Korea were not even a close second.

The Korean War was disastrous for combatants and civilians trapped in the war. The United States signed an armistice at that time to extract itself from the quagmire. It was a humiliating outcome since just a few years earlier, the United States emerged from World War II as a new superpower. The war cost the United States 36,574 deaths[127] and 341 billion dollars (adjusted for 2011 dollars).[128] Many saw the war as a terrible waste of blood and treasure, and they have been trying to push it from their memories. Others wanted to forget it but could not vanquish it from their memories no matter how hard they tried.

Many people strongly felt that someone or some group must be held responsible. They desperately needed a scapegoat. The families of those that fought and died did not tolerate the generals and politicians trying to shift the blame to those that fought in the war and paid the most in terms of hardship and death.

The generals, some of whom were previously seen as heroes for their deeds in WWII, did not want to accept the blame. Never mind that some generals had just been resting on their laurels and basking in the glory of their previous victories in WWII. Additionally, at least one general may have exacerbated the intelligence failure.[129]

The politicians did not want to accept the blame of reducing the military budget after WWII because the public had been clamoring for a peace dividend. With military budgets cut, training and readiness suffered. Military service members on the ground and in the air paid dearly for the mistakes of others.

After a thorough search, a suitable scapegoat was found. Unlike previous military humiliations; however, this scapegoat was not a person or a group of people that could defend themselves from false allegations.

The scapegoat was a new secret weapon the enemy had developed. What was that new secret weapon?

Brainwashing

Yes, brainwashing was to be the scapegoat since no one else would accept the responsibility for losing so much blood and treasure. How can a concept defend itself from false allegation or blame shifting?

Early in the Korean War, "[p]anic spread that China's Communists had learned how to penetrate and control the minds of American prisoners of war."[130] There were many reports of POWs being subjected to "intense psychological conditioning" that made them willing to make false confessions. The CIA suspected that China and Russia had developed brainwashing techniques that were so effective that "human waves" of Chinese and Korean soldiers would "charge to certain death in seemingly inexhaustible numbers."[131]

There was an extensive fear that the American population would soon be brainwashed if these new brainwashing techniques were to continue unchecked.[132] This new phenomenon of brainwashing was not any ordinary propaganda. It was a propaganda on steroids. It was so insidious that it could infect the minds of victims without even realizing they had been brainwashed. They would adamantly—even violently—deny they had been brainwashed in a manner similar to what Plato described in *Allegory of the Cave*[ad][133]

On March 15, 1958, the House of Representatives convened the Committee on Un-American Activities to investigate and document Communist Psychological Warfare (Brainwashing).[134]

Time lines are important. The Korean War raged on from June 25, 1950 to July 27, 1953.

Mr. Edward Hunter was a propaganda specialist (journalist) working for the CIA. He is credited for introducing the new term— brainwashing—to US public on the *Miami News* on September 24, 1950, just three months after the Korean War started. Mr. Hunter alleged that he learned of the idea "in the Far East and Southeast Asia

---

ad   For more information about the prisoners in Pluto's *Allegory of the Cave*, please read the footnote in the Preface section.

during 1950 and 1951," which (at the earliest) would have been just a few months before the Korean War started. Nevertheless, the idea did not gain much traction until a scapegoat was needed.

How did a newspaper reporter in Miami get so far ahead of this story about *brainwashing* very close to the time that the Korean War started? There were reports of POWs being subjected to intensive psychological pressure that surfaced later in the war, but somehow a newspaper reporter from Miami was ahead of the story.

After WWII, the CIA found out Germany had experimented with drugs and hypnosis for interrogation during the war. There were also reports of "amazing results" that were achieved by the Soviets in using "truth drugs." From Congressional hearings in 1977, we see that Project CHATTER was a Navy program that began in the fall of 1947—about the same time that the CIA was founded.

Pavlov Set the Stage

In 1904, Ivan Petrovich Pavlov (1849–1936) was the first Russian to win a Nobel Prize. Although many thought he was a psychologist, he was not by formal training. Instead, he was a physiologist that conducted research on digestion. The associations that he observed between food, sounds, and dogs salivating opened up a vast new field of classical conditioning. From his Nobel Prize citation, we read the following:

> Pavlov's research into the physiology of digestion led him logically to create a science of conditioned reflexes... Experiments carried out by Pavlov and his pupils showed that conditioned reflexes originate in the cerebral cortex... As a result of all this research there emerged an integrated Pavlovian theory on higher nervous activity.[135]

Pavlov's research that revealed some secrets of how the brain works caught the attention of some scientists around the world. However, it was the show trials of the Great Purge (The Great Terror) that caught the attention of Western intelligence agencies. Some hard-core Russian apparatchiks confessed to seemingly impossible crimes.[136] Western intelligence agencies were concerned that Russia had learned the secrets to control the mind due to the extraordinary advances in psychology by Pavlov and his team.

There is no solid evidence that Pavlov did any research on what we recognize as brainwashing. Still, Western intelligence agencies were obsessed to find out if he had. In 1949, Russian (USSR) proxies in Hungary put Cardinal Josef Mindszenty on trial.[137] After watching films and listening to audio recordings of the trial, the CIA issued a Special Security Memorandum declaring "some unknown force had been used on the Cardinal' and speculated that the Hungarian secret police had used 'either hypnosis or drugs, or a combination of the two."[138]

The Committee on Un-American Activities investigated Communist Psychological Warfare (Brainwashing) on March 15, 1958. One of the people testifying at the Congressional hearing was Mr. Edward Hunter. As you may recall from earlier, he was the reporter who wrote a story in the *Miami News* and introduced the American public to the new phenomena of brainwashing.

In 1958, Mr. Hunter's participation in two professions was probably meant to enhance his credibility. Nevertheless, Mr. Hunter's testimony to Congress might leave some with a different impression today than what he intended decades ago. In this era rife with allegations of "Fake News," journalists who boldly announced that they were also propaganda specialists might raise some eyebrows.

COLONEL HEIMLICH: When the war came along, Mr. Hunter, you went into OSS, I understand.

MR. HUNTER: Yes; as a **propaganda specialist**. I call that my sabbatical year -- really 2 [sic] years – away from **journalism**. (Emphasis added.)

To summarize this chapter up to this point, the Korean War was one of many intelligence failures by the fledging CIA within three years of being established. We can attribute these failures to the CIA being blindsided. Paradoxically, as the CIA was obsessed with gathering information about Russian and German mind-control projects, the Korean War broke out. As a result of the Korean War, many military service members were brainwashed.

After the war, the public narrative pushed by the CIA suggested that problems of the Korean War could be blamed on a new secret weapon developed by Russia and used by China and North Korea. This narrative shifted the blame away from the generals and the politicians. Would you expect anything less from some of the best propaganda specialists in the world?

It was pure public relations genius.

Next, we will see how the CIA turned tragedy into a budgetary windfall that would eventually change the world.

Bouncing from Blunders to Bonanzas

The fledging CIA suffered a series of failures.[139] After the Korean War was over, the CIA was plagued with massive resignations and low morale. The agency faced a "rapidly deteriorating situation."[140] Unlike Britain or Russia, the United States did not have an effective intelligence service shortly after WWII.

Lieutenant Colonel Bill Donovan was a hero in WWI, which led to his outsized role in WWII at the rank of major general. Although Major General "Wild Bill" Donovan led the OSS during WWII,[141] the US had to rely heavily on the United Kingdom for intelligence. After WWII, the US was thrust into the position of being a superpower; however, it did not have an intelligence apparatus robust enough to handle the nation's new role as a superpower. Toward the end of WWII, President Roosevelt asked Donovan to propose a plan for a peacetime intelligence agency. When President Roosevelt died, Vice President Truman became the president, and he thought Donovan's plan looked like an American version of the German Gestapo.[142]

Japan signed the Instrument of Surrender on September 2, 1945. Soon thereafter, President Truman "fired Donovan and ordered the OSS to disband in ten days"[143] and the OSS was quickly dissolved on September 20, 1945, which was less than three weeks after Japan formally surrendered. We can get a sense of Truman's extreme distrust of Donovan and the OSS by Truman's ten-day deadline. In a time when travel between continents was predominated by ships, ten days were barely enough time to get personnel—that were serving at locations scattered halfway around the world—back home. Moreover, Truman dissolved the OSS before the last batch of the Japanese military forces surrendered in November 1945. A functional intelligence apparatus and the OSS's robust covert military capabilities would have been very helpful in locating and expediting the surrender of the last batch of Japanese military forces. Later in this book, we will see why Truman may have been in such a hurry to get rid of Donovan and the OSS. Allegedly, Donovan ordered—or at least condoned—dirty tricks[144] that were similar to those allegedly used recently by Jeffrey Epstein for blackmail.[ae]

President Truman's ten-day deadline for dissolving the OSS provided no time to prepare for any possible legacy activity, which was probably just what President Truman wanted. The OSS was superseded by the CIA two years later on September 18, 1947. However, the two-year gap from the OSS to the formation of the CIA had set in motion a chain of events that lead to smartphone addiction and other relevant and notable problems.

As a result of the lack of continuity and loss of highly trained personnel, the "CIA was born with crippling defects."[145] Furthermore, it takes decades to develop spies, spy crafts, and all the institutional supports to run clandestine organizations. The CIA's early efforts to insert spies into other countries were utterly disastrous. "All told, hundreds of the CIA's foreign agents were sent to their death in Russia, Poland, Romania, Ukraine, and the Baltic states."[146]

Like a phoenix rising from the ashes, the CIA turned the blunders of the Korean War into bureaucratic budgetary bonanzas. The result of these bureaucratic maneuvers was a massive infusion of money. In a very short time, the CIA's budget skyrocketed eleven-fold.[147] Because of the repeated failures of trying to gather information by using agents (human intelligence—HUMINT) who were killed by the hundreds, the CIA poured much of the new budgetary windfall into research and technology.

---

ae   Allegedly, Donovan obtained many compromising photographs that he used to blackmail many government officials. Allegedly, Jeffrey Epstein would decades later also obtain many compromising photographs that he used to blackmail many government officials and important business leaders. On Friday August 9, 2019, federal appeals court unsealed about 2,000 pages of documents related to Jeffrey Epstein who was facing charges of sex trafficking involving dozens of underage girls. Epstein was found dead in his jail cell the next morning— Saturday, August 10, 2019.

Before the Korean War, the possibility of brainwashing was known only to a small group of people within the CIA. Because of the terrible, unforgettable outcome of the Korean War, the CIA charged ahead with research into possible brainwashing techniques. The CIA presented brainwashing as an existential threat to the United States. Some alleged that brainwashing would be more useful for conquering a country than using nuclear weapons. Moreover, there would be little or no damage to the national infrastructures as to compare to the situation using explosive armaments and kinetic weapons.

These new threats—real or surreal—provided the justification to conduct research and development of new tools to gather information. Because it lost so many spies and foreign agents, the CIA shifted its emphasis away from human intelligence (HUMINT) to other methods such as aerial photography and electronic methods to gather information that could be turned into intelligence products.

Reoccurring failures in HUMINT resulted in the CIA focusing on technologies that could hoover up vast amounts of raw information. The raw unprocessed pieces of information were to be analyzed and converted into intelligence products. The CIA developed an unquenchable thirst for information. The CIA began developing programs to gather information from all over the world so that it could produce more accurate intelligence products. It also developed a keen eye for dual use technology—a technology that could be used by both the intelligence community and the civilian business sectors. Aerospace, electronics, computer hardware, and software were able to reap huge benefits from the intelligence community.

After the Korean War, the CIA wanted to develop the U-2 spy plane. Apparently, there was interagency competition with the US Air Force over aerial reconnaissance. In 1955, Central Intelligence Agency Officer Richard Bissell showed President Eisenhower aerial photographs of President Eisenhower's favorite golf course—Augusta National Country Club Georgia. Although the photographs were taken from ten miles high, President Eisenhower could see individual golf balls on the greens. President Eisenhower was sold, and the CIA got the job instead of the US Air Force.[148]

The CIA was so flushed with money and was in such a hurry they sent a $1.25 million check to the *home* of Kelly Johnson, chief engineer,[149] for the U-2. That equals to almost twelve million dollars in 2019. How would you like to get a twelve-million-dollar check in your mailbox?

A few years later, the CIA funded the ongoing development of the SR-71 spy plane at a cost of several billion dollars. The CIA had its own air force for spying on other counties. It did not want to be blindsided again and was willing to pay enormous sum of money to prevent any intelligence failures. New technologies needed to build advanced spy planes were one of the specific areas that the CIA wanted to master in a hurry. The SR-71 was designed within a decade of the Korean War. The SR-71 spy plane was in the process of development but was not operational until later in 1966. It set speed records and altitude records that have never been broken. The CIA (and later the Air Force) [af] used the SR-71 for decades and was never shot down. Allegedly, it escaped over 4,000 missiles fired at it.[150] Still, the aircrews had to be very careful when flying their missions to stay just beyond the effective range of ground-to-air missiles. That meant there were some areas that even the SR-71 could not fly over.

Building and operating spy planes have been proven to be extremely expensive. However, the early successes in aerial surveillance gave the CIA a big appetite for mastering expensive technologies, and the CIA was willing to pay a premium for enhanced capabilities. The research and development costs were six hundred million dollars;[151] that is equivalent to over five billion dollars in 2019. Individual planes cost about twenty million dollars in 1960; that is about 173 million dollars each in 2019.[152] The CIA has continued to spend huge amount to master other expensive technologies.

Airplanes can be shot down. So satellites were chosen as the best solution for overhead surveillance to avoid airplanes getting shot down. Yet, rocket technology had not sufficiently matured, hindering the reliability to launch reconnaissance satellites in space orbit. Even when satellites made it into orbit, dropping photographic

---

af   The U-2 and SR-71 airplanes and operations would eventually be transferred from the CIA to the US Air Force.

film pods from reconnaissance satellites to re-enter the atmosphere was unreliably unsuccessful. Developing technology for reliable rockets, reconnaissance satellites, and nonfilm photographs were also extremely expensive.

A secret document written in 1959—and declassified in 2019—laid out the ambitious plans for putting reconnaissance satellites into orbit. Notably, the section titled "Status and Problems" contained a caution, "Project is currently on schedule however project may be jeopardized by lack of funds.[153] Translation—the cost for building and operating on reconnaissance satellites would be out of this world. Securing funding for reconnaissance satellites is also a realistic problem that needed to be solved.

On May 1, 1960—about a year before President Kennedy's speech to Congress—a U-2 spy plane was shot down over Russia. This created an international diplomatic crisis as well as an embarrassment for the outgoing President Eisenhower. Less than a year later, on April 17, 1961, the CIA's failed Bay of Pigs Invasion in Cuba created another political crisis[154] and an international diplomatic crisis.[155] The public was furious. In less than a year, the CIA's fingerprints were all over two failed operations—the U-2 disaster[156] and the Bay of Pigs fiasco.[157] President Kennedy was humiliated.[158]

On April 12, 1961, Russia (USSR) put the first cosmonaut into orbit. Also, about a month after the humiliation over the Bay of Pigs fiasco—on May 25, 1961—President Kennedy gave his famous speech to Congress about going to the moon. His vision and challenge were clear, "We choose to go to the Moon." President Kennedy's speech ignited the imagination of the public, and he became a hero again.

President Kennedy's speech galvanized public support. The resulting public enthusiasm translated into massive government spending to go to the moon.

On July 20, 1969, Neil Armstrong set foot on the moon. It was a very exciting time in American history. The national mood was ecstatic. A few weeks before the moon landing, our family drove several days coast to coast to go to Cape Kennedy as it was known then. (It is since reverted to its original name—Cape Canaveral.) As we toured Cape

Kennedy, we were told of the many off-limit sites on Cape Kennedy because of the "military rockets with classified payloads." Since then, the rocket launches, and payloads have been declassified. The rockets were for the intelligence community, and the payloads were spy satellites.

Before the first astronaut set foot on the moon in 1969, the intelligence community was able to reliably launch reconnaissance satellites into space orbit courtesy of the new technologies developed and paid for by the civilian moonshot project. Declassified document released by the National Reconnaissance Office[159] indicated that the Department of Defense started work on a space plane (Dyna Soar)[ag] [160] in 1957. This document showed an intersection between the rocket technology being developed for reconnaissance and the civilian space technology being developed to put an astronaut on the moon.

The Kennedy speech about going to the moon is often cited as the importance and power of a vision articulated by a leader. Kennedy was credited as being a visionary because of it. Perhaps there may be more to the story. Russia was also working on rockets to put reconnaissance satellites into orbit. The Russian government insisted on a dual program—reconnaissance satellites and cosmonaut space flight. Russian cosmonaut Yuri Gagarin is generally believed to be the first person[ah] into space on April 12, 1961. At forty-seven seconds into video of Yuri Gagarin's heroic homecoming ceremony, it was revealed that the massive cost of the Russian space program suddenly took a back seat when people had a hero and something to ignite their national pride. "There have been grumblings in Russia about the cost of the space program but that is forgotten today as tens of thousands pour into Red Square to get a glimpse of their hero."[161] Did President Kennedy take a cue from the Russians that an excellent way to overcome resistance to an expensive space program was to have a vision about making heroes and sidestepping the astronomical cost of developing reconnaissance satellites?

---

ag   Approved for release as unclassified on February 19, 2019.

ah   The CIA reading library has a paper that cast doubt on the official Russian version "Was Gagarin Really in Space?: Cosmonaut No. 1. A YouTube video offers more details to support allegations that Russian test pilot Vladimir Ilyushin was the first in to space and *Yuri Gagarin Was Not The First Man In Space | Cosmonaut Cover Up | Spark*

Do you think the United States moonshot project was solely about bragging rights to be the first nation to put astronauts on the moon? Alternatively, was the moonshot project a well-orchestrated ~~propaganda~~ public relations campaign by the Mighty Wurlitzer (or a reincarnation of the Mighty Wurlitzer) to encourage the public to pay for expensive new technologies for rockets, satellites, electronics, and computer development? Either way, the moonshot project was very fortuitous for the intelligence community in both timing and development of many new expensive technologies. Google and its new parent company Alphabet still use the term "moonshot projects."[162] In another chapter, we will examine other associations between Google and the intelligence community.

The CIA still puts a premium on technology over spy tradecraft. In a 2013 Senate intelligence report, technical methods of intelligence are emphasized.[ai][163] Furthermore, the CIA is not shy about its sponsorship to several technologies. In fact, several CIA websites highlight how declassified CIA technology has improved our lives. This website is just one example.

> [Y]ou might not be surprised to learn that declassified, publicly released technologies developed by CIA have impacted the world in positive ways. One of the best examples is the common lithium-ion battery, developed by CIA in the 1960s to improve the performance of surveillance equipment and prolong the operation of reconnaissance satellites... The benefits of this declassified technology can be felt close to home today, from its use in pacemakers to your cell phone and digital camera.[164]

In-Q-tel

Many of the technological advancements in smartphones and other smart devices were first envisaged and funded by the CIA. The

---

ai   "Failure to properly resource and use our own R&D to appraise, exploit, and counter the scientific and technical developments of our adversaries—including both state and nonstate actors—may have more immediate and catastrophic consequences than failure in any other field of intelligence.—National Commission for the Review of the Research and Development Programs of the United States Intelligence Community (2013)."

CIA guided these ideas through research and development. After these had matured, many new technologies were launched into commercial success with the help of intelligence agencies funding through a venture capital firm called **In-Q-tel** (IQT).[165]

> IQT was established in 1999 to ensure that our country's intelligence agencies had access to innovative technologies from the startup community to help protect and preserve our nation's security. CIA leaders recognized that technological innovation had largely shifted from the purview of government R&D and large organizations to entrepreneurs and the startup community who were developing much-needed technologies more quickly and less expensively, and continue to do so today.[166]

The CIA is very subtle about placing double meanings and important information in plain sight in a get-it-wink manner. Allegedly, the Q in the middle of the company name is a wink to Q—the person in the movies that introduces James Bond to the fancy high-tech devices. Putting Q in the middle of Intel (short for "intelligence") makes the new name. Since Q symbolizes technology, it is placed in the middle. Therefore, Q is symbolizing that technology is the center of this effort. The name is not Q-Intel or Intel-Q but In-Q-tel. Get it? (Wink!)

According to information provided on the In-Q-tel (IQT) website:

> The significant advantages of IQT's model include:
>
> Rapid product development
>
> Valuable product enhancements
>
> Lower initial and long-term costs to the **national security community** (Emphasis added.)

Have you ever used Google Earth? "Finally, in February 2003, the CIA-funded strategic investor In-Q-Tel made an investment in Keyhole, Inc. Keyhole was a pioneer of interactive 3D earth visualization… CIA worked closely with other Intelligence Community organizations to tailor Keyhole's systems to meet operational needs… The popularity of this technology eventually caught the attention of Google, which acquired Keyhole in 2004. You know this technology today as Google Earth."[167]

TALENT and KEYHOLE

According to a Google news release, "Keyhole's technology combines a multi-terabyte database of mapping information and images collected from satellites and airplanes with easy-to-use software."[168]

The CIA reading library contains a document that was classified in 1964 and recently "Sanitized – Approved for Release" [aj] that states, "TALENT material is the product of U.S. reconnaissance operations from sensitive manned aircraft overflights… KEYHOLE material is the product of U.S. reconnaissance operations from satellites."[169] It may be easy to get the two keyholes confused. KEYHOLE was the name of a previously classified program. Keyhole Corporation is the name of a corporation that developed software for KEYHOLE. Google Inc. acquired Keyhole Corporation, a company in Mountain View, California. Keyhole Corp. was a digital mapping software company that digitalized maps.[170]

The CIA's appetite for information was so enormous that it gathered much more information than it could digest. Its eyes were much bigger than its stomach. It needed better ways to digest and analyze the tsunami of information it was gathering and collating. In the case of satellite photographs, photo analysts in offices—or troops on the ground—had constantly flip from one photograph to the next. They also had to measure distance manually after carefully aligning various maps. Measuring distances was tedious and difficult. Satellite photographs were rarely made to convenient scales such as one inch equals a mile. Manual measurements on satellite photos had to be manually converted using a conversion factor. Slanted photographs—those not taken directly below the satellite or airplane—were even more difficult.[171] [ak] Keyhole Corporation wrote

---

aj   Document Number (FOIA)/ESDN (CREST): CIA-RDP67R00587A000100140024-5

ak   If a photograph was taken at a thirty- or sixty-degree angle from directly down, the distance measurements parallel to the path of the satellite or aircraft were not compressed. However, the distances perpendicular to the path of the satellite or aircraft were compressed and had to be corrected with trigonometry.

software[al] that used databases to stitch photographs from aircraft and satellite together electronically. In addition to making 3D graphical representations, the software has allowed and made measuring distances much easier, and it even allowed users to zoom in and out.

Google was able to buy Keyhole Corporation because it had a large amount of cash. "Google is a search engine company whose growth has brought it to the first rank, and that is growing faster than any of its competitors."[172] This was due in part to a government grant.[173] Fast growth allowed Google to capture a large market share, generate profits, and acquire large amounts of cash. The CIA has been interested in artificial intelligence and has been funding it since at least 1987,[174] and recently, Google has been buying up companies that develop artificial intelligence.[175][176] Do you think it is purely coincidental that Google uses some of its profits to buy companies and technologies that are of interest to the CIA?

The next chapter will look at CIA fronts. Later in this book, we will explore more the various discreet connections between Google and the CIA.

---

al   Keyhole Markup Language (KML) is an XML format for geographic annotations developed by Keyhole, Inc.

CIA Fronts and Proxies

The CIA has a long history of using indirect means of payments and fronts (companies and organizations) around the world. Even through this way, the CIA connection is still concealed.[177] The CIA excels in *opacity* and *deniability*. Thus, it resorted to using front companies or proxies to act on behalf of the CIA. Besides routing money through the DoD for MKULTRA, the CIA used the Society of the Investigation of Human Ecology as another front to fund MKULTRA research.[178] When the CIA built a fleet of SR-71 spy planes (before turning them over to the Air Force), there was not enough titanium in the United States or friendly countries. Undeterred, the CIA set up front companies around the world and bought the titanium from Russia (Soviet Union at the time).[179] The country that sold the titanium to the CIA made it possible to build the plane that would later spy on them.

The CIA ran a covert airline—Air American—for years. If you checkout the online CIA museum, you can see that the CIA now calls Air American "a CIA proprietary airline."[180] This airline front was typical of the many CIA fronts. It provided the CIA the ability to conceal activities and maintain a self-sustaining commercial operation that provided surge capacity when needed.[181]

When Disney wanted to build Disney World in Florida, they realized that if the word got out, the land prices would soar. What did they do? Disney called on retired Major General "Wild Bill" Donovan.

> Starting in the mid-1960s when Disney set out to establish the Disney World Theme Park, they were determined to get land at below market prices... The solution turned out to be cartoon-simple, thanks to the CIA... Disney's key contact was... William "Wild Bill"

Donovan. Sometimes called the "Father of the C.I.A"...
Donovan's attorneys provided fake identities for Disney
agents; they also set up a secret communications center,
and orchestrated a disinformation campaign.[182]

In this quote, you can see several elements that are hallmarks
for the CIA fronts—fake identities, secret communications, and an
orchestrated disinformation campaign. In the case of MKULTRA,
similar tactics were used. The US District Court for the District of
Columbia uncovered that in Orlikow v. United States:[183]

- "Because the Agency funded the research indirectly,
  participating individuals often were unaware of the CIA
  involvement."

- "MKULTRA programs were covert and that the identity of
  the CIA as the funding source was to be kept secret."

We can also see from the 1977 DoD memorandum that the CIA
used the DoD and the US Navy [184] as a front. Therefore, in the rest
of this book, whenever you see something attributed to the Pentagon,
the DoD, or the Navy, you might be correct if you guessed it is the
CIA instead.

Who Was the Genius of Facebook?

D
o you still believe in the tooth fairy?

Do you really believe that a college dropout has come up with a great idea and transformed it into a multibillion-dollar-tech company by himself? Facebook has been mired in controversy since it was founded.[185] [186] *The Accidental Billionaires* (Ben Mezrich, 2009) and *The Social Network* (Columbia Pictures and Relativity Media, 2010) both created a narrative about Mark Zuckerberg. In some popular narratives, Mr. Mark Zuckerberg is referred to as a genius[187] and even elevated him to rock star stature.[188]

Is Mark Zuckerberg really a genius or just a humbug set up by to be a CIA proxy? In 2011, A CBS News article alleged to have established a connection between the CIA and Facebook.[189] Is there any truth to their allegation? Did some reincarnation of the Mighty Wurlitzer[190] create the genius and rock star narratives for Mark Zuckerberg? If a ~~propaganda~~ public relations campaign is successful, many people will believe and defend the narrative instead of the facts. They will become narrative defenders and fact deniers—ND/FD.[am] This behavior is similar to the prisoners in Pluto's Cave. What are the facts regarding Facebook?

Leader Technologies started developing software in 1999[191] that would later be critical for operating Facebook. Court records show "Leader invested 145,000 man-hours and over $10 million to develop the initial concept and build a working embodiment of the technology."

---

am   We can abbreviate this to Narrative Defenders and Fact Deniers or ND/FD. The forward slash indicates that the Narrative Defenders will try to push the narrative over the facts.

[192] Leader Technologies sued Facebook alleging it infringed on Leader Technologies' patent 7,139,761.[193] Moreover, the jury agreed with Leader Technology on that issue. "The jury rendered a verdict that Facebook directly and literally infringed all of the asserted patent claims."[194] However, the jury also rendered a verdict that the patent was invalid [195] because Leader Technologies publicly disclosed the software and offered it for sale more than a year before filing a patent. "A patent is invalid under 35 U.S.C. § 102(b) if the patentee publicly used or offered for sale a product that embodied the patented invention more than one year before filing the patent application."[196]

Before November 5, 2002, Microsoft was working on a system that would have been similar to Facebook if it had continued developing their platform. The Microsoft Research webpage explained that *MyLifeBits* project may still be available from an internet archive.[an] The first webpage captures of Microsoft's *MyLifeBits* project appeared on November 5, 2002, with a summary of the project, including the "MyLifeBits project aims to put all personal documents and media online, to allow time-shifting, and location independence when you are connected to MyLifeBits…articles, books, cards, CDs, letters, memos, papers, photos, pictures, presentations, home movies, videotaped lectures, and voice recordings and stored them digitally."[197]

A few months later (March 20, 2003), the *New York Times* published an article confirming Microsoft's new project. "A small team of Microsoft researchers is devising software for an electronic diary that can keep track of a multitude of everyday details in a person's life -- the e-mail sent, the family photographs taken, the phone calls made, the Web pages visited -- in a single database."[198] Part of the title of this *New York Times* article "Memories as Heirlooms" was very similar to a paper titled "Memories for Life" posted on a DARPA website also in 2003. Some may dismiss that as a mere coincidence. Except "Memories for Life" was part of DARPA's LifeLog project and read as if it was a developmental roadmap for Facebook. More importantly, "Memories for Life" **contained many explicit cautions about safeguarding privacy of personal information**—safeguards that Facebook is now accused of violating continuously.

---

an   MyLifeBits Project, Microsoft Research, Wayback Machine, https://web.archive.org/web/20060207015856/http://research.microsoft.com/barc/mediapresence/mylifebits.aspx

Tracing *MyLifebits* back through the internet archives and various papers and presentations, I detected some revealing comments on a PowerPoint presentation. The title of the second-to-the-last slide of the presentation is "Challenges" and the last line includes these words, "Security, privacy, forgetfulness, **deniability**, etc."[199] (Emphasis added.) It appears that Microsoft decided to steer clear of these challenges.

While Mark Zuckerberg was attending Harvard University, he hacked into the computers of Harvard's computer services department to get photographs of students' faces, which he was not authorized to do.[200] He also hacked two Harvard Crimson reporters' e-mail accounts.[201] The two reporters were looking into a dispute between Zuckerberg and some others people concerning whose idea it was to start HarvardConnection. [202] According to some narratives, HarvardConnection was a forerunner of Facebook. However, Facebook has many similarities to a Defense Advanced Research Projects Agency project called LifeLog. Cameron and Tyler Winklevoss sued Mark Zuckerberg because "The twins originally hired Zuckerberg to work on a dating site for them while at Harvard." The lawsuit was settled out of court and "The twins are believed to have been given 1.2m shares to settle their claim."[203]

Lawrence "Larry" Summers—a former president of Harvard—had a lot to say about the Winklevoss twins.[204] He is quoted in *The blog of The Harvard Crimson* saying "One of the things you learn as a college president is that if an undergraduate is wearing a tie and jacket on Thursday afternoon at 3:00, there are two possibilities... One is that they're looking for a job and have an interview. The other is that they are an asshole... This was the latter case."[205]

Lawrence "Larry" Summers is linked to serial pedophile Jeffrey Epstein.[206] Jeffrey E. Epstein made a $30 million donation to Harvard in 2003. [207] "Indeed, Epstein shares a special connection with one of the most prominent figures at Harvard—University President Lawrence H. Summers... Summers and Epstein serve together on the Trilateral Commission and the Council on Foreign Relations, two elite international relations organizations."[208]

Mark Zuckerberg had dinner with Jeffrey Epstein.[209] Zuckerberg did not dispute the dinner with Jeffrey Epstein. However, a Zuckerberg spokesperson alleges that he did not have any further communication with Jeffrey Epstein.[210] The New York Times cited alleged that Sergey Brin and Larry Page had dinner[211] with the serial pedophile Jeffrey Epstein.

Jeffrey Epstein alleged, "I Collect People, I Own People, I Can Damage People."[212] *The New York Times* published an article alleging Jeffrey Epstein had dirt on "prominent names in technology circles. He said people in Silicon Valley had a reputation for being geeky workaholics, but that was far from the truth: They were hedonistic and regular users of recreational drugs. He said he'd witnessed prominent tech figures taking drugs and arranging for sex."[213]

In July 2019, Jeffrey Epstein was indicted on charges of sex trafficking.[214] Previously, Epstein received an unusually light sentence in a secret plea deal in Florida in 2007.[215] R. Alexander Acosta helped arrange the plea deal. Later Mr. Acosta would become Secretary of Labor in the Trump administration. However, Mr. Acosta resigned in July 2019 because of his work on the Epstein plea deal.[216]

The *Daily Beast* published a story that alleges Epstein to be linked to an intelligence service. Allegedly, Acosta was questioned by President Trump's transition team:

> "Is the Epstein case going to cause a problem [for confirmation hearings]?" Acosta had been asked. Acosta had explained, breezily, apparently, that back in the day he'd had just one meeting on the Epstein case. He'd cut the non-prosecution deal with one of Epstein's attorneys because he had "been told" to back off, that Epstein was above his pay grade. "I was told Epstein 'belonged to intelligence' and to leave it alone," he told his interviewers in the Trump transition, who evidently thought that was a sufficient answer and went ahead and hired Acosta." [217]

Allegations of Epstein's association with intelligence services and blackmail with comprising photography echoed back to allegations of similar activates by OSS under "Wild Bill" Donovan.[218] However, Donovan went on to enjoy his retirement, Epstein did not. On Friday

August 9, 2019, federal appeals court unsealed about 2,000 pages of documents related to Jeffrey Epstein who was facing charges of sex trafficking involving dozens of underage girls. [219] Epstein was found dead in his jail cell the next morning—Saturday, August 10, 2019.

Did some reincarnation of the Mighty Wurlitzer prevent the airing of the information Amy Robach gathered from Virginia Roberts? Jeffrey Epstein appears to have been protected by other powerful people. 20/20 co-anchor Amy Robach alleges that she interviewed Virginia Roberts and "had the story for three years." Robach claims ABC refused to air the details, "We would not put it on the air." [220]

Less than two weeks later, Journalist Megyn Kelley broke the story and tweeted:

> MK EXCLUSIVE: House Minority Leader Kevin McCarthy turns up heat on ABC: demands answers about why they spiked the Epstein story. McCarthy to ABC News Pres. James Goldston: "I am deeply concerned that ... ABC News chose to bury the truth." [221]

— Megan Kelly November 17, 2019

From ABC News website, we can see a connection or ABC News and The Walt Disney Company:

ABC News is the news gathering and broadcasting division of the American Broadcasting Company, a subsidiary of The Walt Disney Company. Its flagship program is *World News with Diane Sawyer*; other programs include morning show *Good Morning America*, *Nightline*, television news magazine shows *Primetime* & *20/20*...[222]

As we saw a few pages above:

Starting in the mid-1960s when Disney set out to establish the Disney World Theme Park, they were determined to get land at below market prices... The solution turned out to be cartoon-simple, thanks to the CIA... Disney's key contact was... William "Wild Bill" Donovan. Sometimes called the "Father of the C.I.A"... Donovan's attorneys provided fake identities for Disney agents; they also set up a secret communications center, and orchestrated a disinformation campaign.[223]

Any possible connections between Jeffrey Epstein, ABC News, Disney, and "Wild Bill" Donovan are probably just coincidental.

Is There Any Connection Between the CIA and Facebook?

In 2003, "Memories for Life" was posted on DARPA LifeLog website. "Memories for Life" **clearly pointed out many privacy problems social media platforms would encounter**. The Belgium Privacy Protection Commission—working with German, Dutch, French, and Spanish counterparts—accused Facebook of trampling over privacy laws.[224] Facebook dismissively blamed the problem on a "bug."[225]

Facebook has a pattern of breaking its privacy promises. In 2011, the Federal Trade Commission (FTC) and Facebook reached an agreement on privacy violations—"Facebook Settles FTC Charges That It Deceived Consumers By Failing To Keep Privacy Promises"[226]

- In December 2009, Facebook changed its website so certain information that users may have designated as private—such as their Friends List—was made public. They didn't warn users that this change was coming, or get their approval in advance.

- Facebook represented that third-party apps that users' installed would have access only to user information that they needed to operate. In fact, the apps could access nearly all of users' personal data—data the apps didn't need.

- Facebook told users they could restrict sharing of data to limited audiences—for example with "Friends Only." In fact, selecting "Friends Only" did not prevent their information from being shared with third-party applications their friends used.

- Facebook had a "Verified Apps" program & claimed it certified the security of participating apps. It didn't.

- Facebook promised users that it would not share their personal information with advertisers. It did.

- Facebook claimed that when users deactivated or deleted their accounts, their photos and videos would be inaccessible. But

Facebook allowed access to the content, even after users had deactivated or deleted their accounts.

- Facebook claimed that it complied with the U.S.- EU Safe Harbor Framework that governs data transfer between the U.S. and the European Union. It didn't.

Facebook agreed to be bound by a twenty-year consent decree imposed by the FTC. Facebook agreed to "[e]stablish and implement, and thereafter maintain...a comprehensive privacy program that is reasonably designed to (1) address privacy risks related to the development and management of new and existing products and services for consumers, and (2) protect the privacy and confidentiality of covered information."

Many continue to support Mark Zuckerberg because Facebook is profitable. In their rush to support Zuckerberg, some even alleged he was a genius. However, the real genius was born in 1901, over eight decades before Mark Zuckerberg was born.

Paul Lazarsfeld, PhD

Few people have heard of Paul Lazarsfeld, PhD. He is the real genius behind Facebook. Dr. Lazarsfeld earned a doctorate in mathematics with a dissertation that covered mathematical aspects of Einstein's theory of gravity. Using his intellectual prowess in mathematics, he co-founded what sounds like a very odd mixture—mathematical sociology. He was known for bringing the "psychology approach" to the study of consumer behavior.

Dr. Lazarsfeld pioneered modern advertising. Without his work, there would be no social media, as we know it today. Mathematical sociology provides the revenue that makes Facebook "free" to users. The service is free to users because marketers benefit from the information and very accurate inferences that may be gleaned by analyzing users' online behavior and posts.

Dr. Paul F. Lazarsfeld was a psychology instructor at Vienna University. In 1930, Dr. Lazarsfeld moved to the United States, and in 1934, he soon published "The Psychological Aspects of Market

Research" in the *Harvard Business Review*. Lazarsfeld also cofounded the field of mathematical sociology, as mentioned previously.

Mathematical sociology has become part of several disciplines including social network analysis. It is now a powerful way to mine vast amount of information from social network websites and has become very useful for some government agencies. For example, the Department of Homeland Security is *"Using Social Media to Analyze, Thwart Terrorist Activity."*[227]

Dr. Lazarsfeld pioneered mathematical methods for harvesting vast amounts of information from social networking sites long before Zuckerberg was born. All Zuckerberg needed to succeed was for the price of computers and memory to drop and for someone to develop a large database of people. Computers and algorithms electronically can stitch together very detailed dossiers on people by linking thousands of seemly insignificant pieces of information gathered from personal social media accounts.

If Mark Zuckerberg is not the genius that some sycophants allege and Dr. Lazarsfeld died before Facebook was founded, who else was behind the Facebook phenomena?

LifeLog→February 4, 2004→Facebook?

A CBS News article alleged to have established a connection between the CIA and social media.[228] By using Defense Advanced Research Projects Agency (DARPA) webpages, we can trace the development of Lifelog[ao]—a program that has many similarities to Facebook. We have seen in previous chapters several instances in which the CIA used front companies. Do you think the intelligence community might have used the Pentagon as a front to hide their connection to Facebook? You may get a more realistic view of Lifelog if you substitute *CIA* or *intelligence community* for *military, commanders,* or *Pentagon* in the following excerpts.

> The research is designed to extend the model of a personal digital assistant (PDA) to one that might eventually become a personal digital partner… LifeLog is a program that steps towards that goal. The LifeLog Program addresses a targeted and very difficult problem: how individuals might capture and analyze their own experiences, preferences and goals. The LifeLog capability would provide an electronic diary to help the individual more accurately recall and use his or her past experiences to be more effective in current. [229]

How might this information be used?

LifeLog technology will be useful in several different ways. First, the technology could result in far more

---

ao   DARPA has deleted the previous webpages on Lifelog. It might still be available at https://web.archive.org/web/20040331065003/http://www.nesc.ac.uk/esi/events/Grand_Challenges/proposals/Memories.pdf .

effective computer assistants for warfighters and commanders because the computer assistant can access the user's past experiences. [230]

The DARPA's LifeLog webpage lists five references but only the last one is of importance to us—UK CRC Grand Challenge "Memories for Life" (2003) [ap] This paper was written by Andrew Fitzgibbon

---

[ap] Copyright notice. "This is a work of the U.S. Government and is not subject to copyright protection in the United States. Foreign copyrights may apply." Answer to question 318, https://www.cendi.gov/publications/04-8copyright.html#318
"Copyright protection is not provided for U.S. Government works under U.S. Copyright Law. Therefore, there is no U.S. Copyright to be transferred. U.S Government employees should inform the publisher of their employment status and should not sign any document purporting to transfer a U.S. copyright as a prerequisite to publication."
"Substantial quotations" are included in the text since Facebook violated privacy promises many times. Mark Zuckerberg had to testify to Congress about privacy, and Facebook was fined by the Federal Trade Commission and subject to further restriction in the future. These substantial quotations are necessary to establish clearly that many privacy concerns were raised in 2003 under LifeLog. The plethora of privacy concern needed to be addressed with Criticism and Commentary.
Although these quotations are substantial, they are allowed under "fair use" even if the material was copyrighted, which it is not. The paper 2003 "Memories for Life" was posted without any copyright notifications for several months on a government website (DARPA's website for Lifelog) as part of a government-funded project. Therefore, it is considered a "government work" under copyright laws and regulations. Some might argue that the authors, Andrew Fitzgibbon and Ehud, might be considered contractors, thus being eligible for copyright protection for their 2003 paper. However, Chapter 4 of *Frequently Asked Questions About Copyright* clarifies this issue. Under paragraph 4.1 (If a work was created under a government contract, who holds the copyright?), it states, "Under the FAR general data rights clause (FAR 52.227-14), except for works in which the contractor asserts claim to copyright, the Government has unlimited rights in all data first produced in the performance of a contract and all data delivered under a contract unless provided otherwise in the contract."
There is no evidence that the authors of "Memories for Life" asserted any claims for copyright. Their paper was posted on a government website (Defense Advanced Research Project Agency) without any copyright notifications for many months. According to FAR in paragraph 4.3, "the contractor must place a copyright notice acknowledging the government sponsorship (including contract number) on the work…If no copyright notice is placed on the work, the Government obtains unlimited rights in the work." Thus, Andrew Fitzgibbon and Ehud Reiter—the authors of "Memories for Life"—forfeited any copyright protection to their 2003 paper.
If anyone minimizes the arguments above, several court rulings have set legal precedent that "[e]ven substantial quotations may constitute fair use in commenting on a published work." The United States District Court for the Northern District of California, Michael Savage v. Council on American-Islamic Relations found that using significant portions of original material is sometimes warranted for criticism and commentary as explained, "17 U.S.C. § 107(3). This factor looks to the quantity and significance of the material used to determine whether the use is reasonably necessary to accomplish the purpose of the defendant's work and whether it supersedes or constitutes the heart of the original work. *Campbell*, 510 U.S. at 586-87. In addition, **the Supreme Court has considered the persuasiveness of the critic's justification for the copying based on the first fair use factor, because the Court recognizes that the extent of permissible copying varies with the purpose and character of the use. Id. Even**

and Ehud Reiter in May 2003. [231] If you read the entire eight-page document, you will see many parallels of what is described in this paper and what Facebook has become. It also contains several warnings about privacy and public acceptance including some prescient statements. (Emphasis had been added. Some words appear to be misspelled. I chose to leave them in original British English instead of correcting to American English.)

> This tsunami of data presents numerous challenges to computer science, including: how to physically store such "digital memories" over decades; how to **protect privacy**, especially when data such as **photos may involve more than one person**. How can we **protect people's privacy** ... significant risk is perhaps **public hostility** if the privacy implications are not carefully addressed ... public policy issues which must be addressed.
>
> - conflict with commercial objectives
> - control and access rights
>
> People **may be hostile** to this challenge unless they feel confident that they have sufficient **control over their memories**.
>
> Significant risk is perhaps **public hostility** if the privacy implications are not carefully addressed.
>
> Also the challenge of rigorously **proving to a skeptical** [*sic*] **public that their memories are secure from hackers, amoral companies, and "Big Brother"** [sic] **governments**. These are just a few of the scientific challenges of "Memories for Life."
>
> Memories for Life also **raises public policy issues which must be addressed, in particular about control and access rights**. For example, should courts

---

substantial quotations may constitute fair use in commenting on a published work may constitute fair use in commenting on a published work." (Emphasis added.)
"Memories for Life" was archived at https://web.archive.org/web/20040331065003/http:/www.nesc.ac.uk/esi/events/Grand_Challenges/proposals/Memories.pdf "Substantial quotations" are included in this text in case readers are unable to access it.

or the police have the right to access memories that are relevant to a legal case or criminal investigation? **Should people who are included in another person's memories (in a digital photograph, for example) have any control over how these memories are used?** Should aggregate information from memories be made available for medical and other kinds of scientific research? Such issues must be resolved in a way that is satisfactory to the community.

Security: How can we **protect people's privacy**, especially when one person's "memories" contain information about someone else? What **control** should people have over information about them in other people's memories, and **how can this control be implemented**? How can we prove both to the scientific community and to the general public that **memories are secure from attackers?**

Certainly the amount of media attention received by **Microsoft's MyLifeBits** project suggests that the media consider this topic to be of widespread interest.

Microsoft in particular is also working on longer-term research in this area, in the MyLifeBits project mentioned above. We welcome the interest of Microsoft and other companies in this area. [232]

The *New York Times* Sounded the Alarm but Few Listened

In 2003, the *New York Times* published a Reuter's article titled "Pentagon Explores a New Frontier In the World of Virtual Intelligence."[233]

The Pentagon is shopping for ways to capture everything a person sees... The projected system, called LifeLog, would take in all of a subject's experience, from phone numbers dialed and e-mail messages viewed to every breath taken, step made and place gone. The idea is to index the material and make patterns easily retrievable.

Many Did Their Homework. Maybe One Did Not

Did many potential participants of Lifelog do their homework? Did they carefully read page 2 of "Memories for Life"—a paper written in 2003 by Andrew Fitzgibbon and Ehud Reiter? Page 2 dealt with problems of skeptical public, privacy issues, public policy, etc. In this paper, Fitzgibbon and Reiter wrote, "We welcome the interest of Microsoft and other companies in this area." Microsoft quietly launched a social network program and then quietly shut it down in 2011.[234] Microsoft's research in social media was listed in as footnote number 1 in "Memories for Life."[aq] The Microsoft Research webpage explaining *MyLifeBits* project may still be available from an internet archive.[ar]

Again, timelines are important. Fitzgibbon and Reiter published their paper May 22, 2003, which pointed out many red flags concerning privacy and public policy. About nine months later, the Pentagon killed the LifeLog Project[235] on February 4, 2004—the same day Facebook was founded.[236] Coincidence? (Wink!)

Governments can purchase your private information from data brokers just as corporations can. As the World Privacy Forum noted, Government Reliance on Commercial Databases has Few Legal Limits[237] Why risk the bad publicity for the Pentagon or CIA if you could shift role of gathering information to a corporation that would act as a front or a proxy?

Many people still believe that their privacy is protected by both the Privacy Act of 1974 and the Health Insurance Portability and Accountability Act of 1996. However, data brokers found clever ways to get around laws and regulations. For example, they do not use names or social security numbers. Instead, they use a wide variety of other identifying characteristics. For example, telephone numbers have largely replaced social security numbers. Alternatively, they can use a combination of characteristics about an individual that makes them unique among billions of other people. For example, you would

---

aq   "Memories for Life" https://web.archive.org/web/20040331065003/http:/www.nesc.ac.uk/esi/events/Grand_Challenges/proposals/Memories.pdf

ar   MyLifeBits Project, Microsoft Research, Wayback Machine https://web.archive.org/web/20060207015856/http://research.microsoft.com/barc/mediapresence/mylifebits.aspx

not need to know the pirate's name if you knew the pirate had several unique characteristics such as the following:

- a patch over his left eye
- a specific set of colorful tattoos on specific locations of his body
- height
- hair color
- birthday
- a specific dental pattern of missing teeth
- earrings in both ears or an earring in one ear or the other
- a wooden leg on his right leg
- a hooked arm on his left arm
- a parrot that usually sits on his left shoulder so the pirate could feed it treats with his right hand

Is Mark Zuckerberg behaving like a lawless pirate and stealing your private information? You can decide for yourself.

The Other Genius of Facebook

The media has lionized Mark Zuckerberg as the genius of Facebook.[238] Is there any hard evidence to support that notion, or is it just media hype? What college dropout apparently did not read—or heed—the numerous cautions spelled out in detail in the 2003 paper, "Memories for Life" written by Andrew Fitzgibbon and Ehud Reiter for DARPA's LifeLog project? [239] In contrast, who made a huge profit on Facebook without being compelled to testify in front of Congress for problems forewarned in "Memories for Life"?

Mark Zuckerberg and Peter Thiel are both billionaires. Mark Zuckerberg dropped out of college and has no college degree (other than an honorary degree largely due to the commercial success of Facebook). Peter Thiel scored first in a California-wide mathematics test while attending public school in San Mateo.[240] If you recall, Dr. Paul Lazarsfeld, who founded mathematical sociology also excelled in mathematics. He earned a doctorate in mathematics with a dissertation that covered mathematical aspects of Einstein's theory of gravity.

Peter Thiel studied at Stanford earning a bachelor of arts in philosophy[241] and then a law degree (juris doctor) from Stanford Law

School.[242] He then clerked for Judge James Larry Edmondson, Senior United States Circuit Judge of the United States Court of Appeals for the Eleventh Circuit.[243] Following the clerkship, Peter Thiel worked for a very prestigious law firm—Sullivan & Cromwell.[244] Sullivan & Cromwell recently earned two "Best Law Firm of the Year" awards and twenty-six national tier one ratings.[245]

Allen Dulles authorized Project MKULTRA in 1953[246] and he later became the director of the CIA. In addition to working for the government, Allen Dulles was a lawyer and partner of Sullivan & Cromwell.[247] That is the same law firm where Peter Thiel worked before he got in on the ground floor of both PayPal and Facebook. You can decide for yourself if any of these coincidences are important.

Peter Thiel founded PayPal. He then went on to be co-founder and chairman of Palantir,[248] which is a big data analytics company. *The Guardian*—a British daily newspaper—alleges that Palantir is a CIA-backed start up and "Palantir: the 'special ops' tech giant that wields as much real-world power as Google."[249] You can read their article and decide for yourself if their allegations have merit. Regarding Palantir, Bloomberg (a financial, software, data, and media company) states, "Palantir Knows Everything About You… Founded in 2004 by Peter Thiel and some fellow PayPal alumni, Palantir cut its teeth working for the Pentagon and the CIA in Afghanistan and Iraq."[250]

Peter Thiel was the first big investor of Facebook[251] and invested $500,000 that was converted to 10.2 percent of Facebook stock.[252] This also made Peter Thiel a member of Facebook's board. [253] A March 27, 2018, *New York Times* article (*Spy Contractor's Idea Helped Cambridge Analytica Harvest Facebook Data*) explains how Palantir obtained social network data from Facebook.[254]

The CIA has had to testify to Congress many times for their bad behavior, misdeeds, and attempts to hide unsavory activities from the public. Recall a statement by a CIA Inspector General.[255]

> Precautions must be taken not only to protect operations from exposure to enemy forces but also to conceal these activities from the American public in general. The knowledge that the Agency is engaging

in unethical and illicit activities would have serious repercussions in political and diplomatic circles and would be detrimental to the accomplishment of its mission.

Do you think the CIA realized the potential problems that would lie ahead and found a college kid that did not do his homework to be the fall guy? Do you think the CIA found a proxy that would eventually have to testify in front of Congress[256] when things blew up as forewarned by Andrew Fitzgibbon and Ehud Reiter in their 2003 paper? It is called plausible denial. This is an area where the CIA excels.

Premediated Fraud or Negligence—"No Expectations of Privacy"

O
n March 6, 2019, Facebook posted "A Privacy-Focused Vision for Social Networking"[257] on its website that "promised a privacy-friendly Facebook, sort of"[258] and it did not take long for Mark Zuckerberg to break that promise. Nine days later, on March 15, 2019, Facebook's lawyers filed a Motion to Dismiss Amended Complaint[259] in the United States District Court for the Northern District of California for dismal. What was their basis for requesting the *Facebook, Inc. Consumer Privacy User Profile Litigation* be dismissed?

Facebook blamed users for destroying their expectation of privacy.[260] You read that correctly. Facebook lawyers allege Facebook users have no expectation of privacy. Orin Snyder of Gibson Dunn & Crutcher is defending Facebook in this lawsuit. Snyder alleged users by their own actions have destroyed any expectation of privacy.[261] That is *very* rich. You can read the courtroom discussions on the court transcripts.[262]

Recall that the Pentagon killed the LifeLog project[263] on February 4, 2004—the same day Facebook was founded. [264] Then, several years later, Facebook went public and sold stock. In order to sell stock in public equity markets, Facebook filed Form S-1 with the Securities Exchange Commission (SEC) on February 1, 2012. On pages 2 and 73 of this form, Facebook states, "Through Facebook's privacy and sharing settings, our users can control what they share and with whom they share it."[265] Those were the statements made to the public when Facebook sold stock. Given what history has proven about Facebook's disregard for privacy, did Facebook deliberately plan beforehand to misrepresent its plans? Did Facebook comment fraud when it filed the initial papers with the Securities Exchange Commission?

There are two unusual statements in bold red letters on the first page of Form S-1 that follows the SEC cover page. This begs a question: Why did the SEC allow Facebook to go public with an incomplete Form S-1? (Emphasis added below.)

> **The information in this prospectus is not complete and may be changed.** (This statement is in red letters in the official on-line document.)

> **The information in this preliminary prospectus is not complete and is subject to change.**

> *This summary is not complete and does not contain all of the information you should consider...*

> PROSPECTUS *(Subject to Completion)*... Dated February 1, 2012 (This statement is in red italics letters in the original on-line document.)

Is it a premeditated fraud or negligence that Mark Zuckerberg and Facebook **did not inform SEC** about LifeLog and privacy problems previously identified in "Memories for Life"? These should have been included as "Risks." Were investors adequately informed about the risks that were clearly explained in "Memories for Life"?

Is it a premeditated fraud or negligence that Facebook **did not inform the US District Court for the Northern District of California** about LifeLog and privacy problems previously identified in "Memories for Life"?

Is it a premeditated fraud or negligence that Mark Zuckerberg and Facebook **did not inform the public** about LifeLog and privacy problems previously identified in "Memories for Life"? If so, does it open up new avenues for a new class action lawsuit against Mark Zuckerberg? Can people claw back his private wealth if it was obtained by fraud?

I believe it would be very insightful if lawyers could question Mark Zuckerberg in a sworn testimony about any communications he had with DARPA, the Pentagon, the CIA, or others in the intelligence community. Mark Zuckerberg should testify about his knowledge of LifeLog or "Memories for Life."

Do you think that if Mark Zuckerberg knew about "Memories for Life," he should have informed both the SEC and the US District Court for the Northern District of California? On the other hand, if Mark Zuckerberg was not aware of "Memories for Life," (which was available for public viewing for several years), do you think he failed his duties as president and CEO of Facebook to protect users and investors?

Before answering those questions, one should consider Mark Zuckerberg's mind-set. Consider the following text messages in which a friend asked Mark Zuckerberg how he got information.[266]

> FRIEND: what!? how'd you manage that one?
> ZUCK: they "trust me"
> ZUCK: dumb f*cks (Ed. The original text did not contain an asterisk.)

Second, Mark Zuckerberg appears to be very aggressive. Consider one of his statements, "**Move fast and break things. Unless you are breaking stuff, you are not moving fast enough**."[267] (Emphasis added.)

Is Facebook's strategy to promise privacy while Facebook's lawyers fight rear-guard actions in court over broken promises? Privacy lawsuits have been piling up for years and yet Mark Zuckerberg continues to make more promises—and Facebook makes more profits. In 2019, there were sixteen pending lawsuits against Facebook for privacy infarctions.[268] That is just in the United States. Over 11,000 people in Europe sued Facebook in 2014.[269] Some lawsuits are dismissed others result in fines. In 2018, Facebook lost a legal case in Belgium and was ordered to pay €250,000 a day until it complies with EU privacy laws.[270] In 2017, Facebook fined €1.2M (about $1.4 million) for privacy violations in Spain[271] and €110m by the EU.[272]

On July 24, 2019, the Federal Trade Commission fined Facebook $5 billion.[273] In addition to the record setting fine, the FTC imposed many sweeping new requirements:

> Facebook CEO Mark Zuckerberg and designated compliance officers must independently submit to

the FTC quarterly certifications that the company is in compliance with the privacy program mandated by the order, as well as an annual certification that the company is in overall compliance with the order. Any false certification will subject them to individual civil and criminal penalties.

It establishes an independent privacy committee of Facebook's board of directors, removing unfettered control by Facebook's CEO Mark Zuckerberg over decisions affecting user privacy. Members of the privacy committee must be independent and will be appointed by an independent nominating committee.

The FTC imposed a new 20-year settlement order on Facebook.[274] Facebook is finally facing a modicum regulatory accountability. However, it still appears to be out of control.

Snopes, an alleged fact-checker, acknowledged that Facebook was listening to your conversations *"but it doesn't record your personal conversations."* (Emphasis added.) [275] Facebook said that they "only accesses users' microphone if the user has given our app permission and if they are actively using a specific feature that requires audio (like voice messaging features)."[276] However, Facebook filed a patent application that can detect what broadcasts you are listening to or watching.[277] On August 13, 2019, Bloomberg reported, "Facebook Inc. has been paying hundreds of outside contractors to transcribe clips of audio from users of its services."[278] This was after Zuckerberg testified to Congress that Facebook does not listen. "You're talking about this conspiracy theory that gets passed around that we listen to what's going on on [sic] your microphone and use that for ads," Zuckerberg told US Senator Gary Peters in April 2018. '*We don't do that.*'" (Emphasis added.)[279]

On November 12, 2019, The Next Web published a story titled *Facebook is secretly using your iPhone's camera as you scroll your feed.*[280] The bug was found by Joshua Maddux:

Found a @facebook #security & #privacy issue. When the app is open it actively uses the camera. I found a bug in the app that lets you see the camera open behind your feed. Note that I had the camera pointed at the carpet. pic.twitter.com/B8b9oE1nbl

— Joshua Maddux (@JoshuaMaddux) November 10, 2019

On November 13, 2019, Facebook acknowledge the problem calling it a bug. [281]

Do you think you can trust Facebook? If not, are there any legal remedies available?

Are Legal Remedies Available?

I am not an attorney. In fact, my understanding of the law is rather simplistic. I understand that if I am speeding and fined for speeding, I must pay the fine. If I do not pay the fine, I am subject to being arrested. Similarly, I understand that if I am driving a vehicle and run over someone, then I am subject to both criminal and civil (tort) actions.

Drug dealers that sell illegal addictive drugs are arrested and tried in court. If the courts find them guilty, they put them in prison, and the government confiscates their assets. For too long, there has been a two-tiered justice system. Drug dealers are often punished for enabling dopamine-associated, addictive behavior. Yet, tech companies and tech billionaires have amassed fortunes from dopamine-associated, addictive behavior without any consequences.

If I engage in business and commit fraud, I can be charged with criminal offenses and fined monetary penalties. If Mark Zuckerberg has promised privacy and then broke it, do you think he should be criminally charged with fraud and forced to pay monetary fines to those he defrauded?

Nicotine and Opioid Litigation

Nicotine is addictive. The tobacco companies knew it for a long time. Yet, for many years, they continued to place profits ahead of the public's well-being. They also waged a long legal battle to drag out lawsuits for years. In early lawsuits, the tobacco companies placed the blame on individuals. The tobacco companies also donated large sums of money to politicians and became very cozy with politicians and

73

regulators. Finally, after many years, the legal tide turned when leaked documents showed that the tobacco companies knew the addictive nature of tobacco.[282]

OxyContin is addictive. Yet, for many years, they continued to place profits ahead of the public's well-being. They also waged long legal battles and drag out lawsuits for years. According to the *New York Times* and the *Wall Street Journal,*

> Manufacturers funded "front groups" that were "disguised as 'unbiased' sources of cutting-edge medical research and information… Physicians were paid as consultants to further spread their message. The companies claimed that opioids were safer than high doses of acetaminophen and other anti-inflammatory agents and that there was a minuscule risk of addiction."[283]

> Purdue Pharma, the maker of OxyContin, and its owners, the Sackler family, agreed to pay $270 million to avoid going to a state court trial over the company's role in the opioid addiction epidemic that has killed more than 200,000 Americans over the past two decades.[284]

Johnson & Johnson was ordered to pay $572.1 million to the state of Oklahoma for using deceptively marketing of addictive opioid painkillers.[285] Opioids activate dopamine neurons that activate the almonds (amygdala) and the pleasure reward center of the brain.[286] Therefore, dopamine is one-step closer to the almonds (amygdala) than opioids. It is noteworthy that "Oklahoma state court judge Thad Balkman said, the state proved Johnson & Johnson launched a misleading marketing campaign to convince the public that opioids posed little addiction risk."[287]

An editorial in the *Wall Street Journal* included in the byline "*The $572 million ruling greatly expands product liability tort law*"[288] Will this ruling open the door for lawsuits against tech companies and tech billionaires that—according to many insiders—deliberative designed smartphones, apps, and social media to be addictive?

Like the tobacco companies, tech companies, app developers, social media, and vendors of video games have known for years about dopamine's role in addictive behavior. Dopamine plays a very important role in addiction whether it is initiated by drugs (e.g., cocaine, amphetamines, nicotine, etc.) or electronic devices (e.g., smartphones and gaming videos). Why are tech companies, app developers, social media, and vendors of video games allowed to put profits ahead of public well-being like the tobacco companies and pharmaceutical companies were able to do for such a long time?

In addition to addiction, there are many documented mental and physical problems that resulted from smartphone and video gaming addiction. There are so many that I will not attempt to list all of them here. If pharmaceutical companies advertise drugs, they have to list the possible side effects. If they advertised *dopamine* for IV use, they have to list the possible side effects too. However, tech companies can manipulate your brain to release *dopamine* to stimulate your pleasure/reward system without telling you of any possible side effects. Why are tech companies not liable to the same standards as pharmaceutical companies?

How long will the public allow tech companies, app developers, and vendors of video games to exploit a two-tiered system of justice? A few reap fantastic profits while many pay the price physically, financially, emotionally, and socially. People and companies that behave like parasites have knowingly exploited dopamine to amass wealth. Furthermore, they cleverly exploited dopamine research by the CIA's mind-control program. The CIA mind-control research was meant to **PROTECT** the public from foreign agents not to **EXPLOIT** the public. (Emphasis added.) Has the time come to redistribute some of that dopamine-derived wealth? The government can seize assets of drug dealers that also exploit dopamine to amass wealth. Should people be able claw back some wealth amassed by parasitic tech companies and billionaires that exploit dopamine?

These facts may justify new class-action lawsuits. The litigation should be straightforward. Courts have established legal precedence in tobacco and opioid litigation. Judges and juries held that companies cannot place all the blame for addiction on addicted individuals.

Courts held companies liable when it was proven they knew about addiction and yet promoted addictive behaviors for profits.[289]

Why Should Dopamine Be Treated Differently Than Nicotine or Opioids?

What about someone that is injured or killed by a driver that was distracted by texting or browsing on social media using his smartphone? It is already well established that drivers are distracted by their cell phones (and smartphones by extension).[290] The Department of Transportation already has data on the number of fatalities that[291] are caused by cell phones (and smartphones by extension).

I am not a fan of lawsuits. Do you think Facebook and other tech companies are out of control and deliberately dangerous? Do you think it is time for some smart lawyers to hold smartphone designers, manufactures, social media, and app designers accountable for death, injury, and property damages? Do you think the legal doctrine of "Proximate Cause" and "Substantial Effect"[292] might be applicable?

Companies that design smartphones and apps deliberately design them to provide users with dopamine squirts that cause addiction. Smartphone designers could have designed smartphones to be safer and discourage (or prevent) smartphone use that might distract drivers. However, they did not.

In 2014, texting is responsible for an estimated five percent of crashes.[293] It is probably higher now. Smartphones are smart enough to know if someone might be driving. Smartphones using Google's Android operating system and Apple's iOS operating system gather incredible amounts of information about people from their smartphones. Dr. Douglas C. Schmidt is a professor of engineering (Computer Science), Associate Provost of Research, and Data Science Institute codirector at Vanderbilt University. Dr. Schmidt brought to light that Android smartphones send 11.9 MB of information back to Google servers about individual users every day. Likewise, Apple smartphones sent back 1.4 MB back to Apple servers every day.[294]

Google, Apple, and Facebook have enough information about individuals, and they are smart enough to know if they are more likely to take public transportation, use ride-sharing services like Uber or Lyft ™, be a passenger in a car, or drive a car. Smartphones have accelerometers and GPS-tracking devices that can easily detect whether someone is using their smartphone while they are moving.

Google and Apple software engineers could have easily designed features that would actively discourage drivers from texting using their smartphones while driving or even suspend smartphone operations while driving. They could have incorporated features to stop the audible tones that have conditioned people to check their smartphones. Smartphones could have functions like to automatically respond to text messages with a message such as, "The person you are trying to reach is driving now and cannot be disturbed. They will get your text message as soon as they stop and get out of the car."

Google, Apple, and Facebook could have included safety interventions such as "Motion Detected. Are you driving while using this smartphone?" If the person is normally a driver but they are a passenger this time, they could respond, "No, I am not driving." Such safety interventions would be very easy to program, yet Google, Apple, and Facebook have not yet taken the extra step to prevent smartphones from distracting drivers or differentiating between drivers and passengers.

After this book is published and these safety suggestions are made public, do you think Google, Apple, and Facebook should be held liable by "Proximate Cause" and "Substantial Effect"[295] if an innocent person is injured or killed by drivers who are distracted by their smartphones?

Researchers have established—and many former insiders have admitted—that Facebook and other companies deliberately use dopamine to make apps and social media addictive and induce anxiety if ignored.[296, 297, 298, 299] For many years, tobacco companies tried to place all the blame of addiction exclusively on the addicted individual. However, courts eventually determined that those that profited from the addiction should also be held accountable for continuous encouragement of addiction. Why should tech companies and tech billionaires get away with profiting from addiction after legal precedence has already been set that addictions are not exclusively the fault of the addicted individual?

Did the Intelligence Community Hatch Google When the Time Was Right?

Do you still believe in Santa Claus?

Do you believe that two college kids—all by themselves—had a great idea, started a company in a garage,[300] and then turned Google into a multibillion-dollar company?

Unlike the Santa Claus question, the latter question is partially true. However, there are a lot more to the Google story. Google is closely associated with the internet and smartphones. However, one writer opines, "The company called Google has turned itself into a generic metaphor for our politicized times."[301] There may be a small twist of irony in that statement since Google has been associated—by some—with the CIA, which often finds itself in the center of political controversies. Even with the help of journalist-propaganda specialists like Mr. Edward Hunter, who can help shape narratives, political controversies swirl around the CIA and companies associated with it. Are Larry Page and Sergey Brin geniuses or just humbugs set up by the CIA to be proxies?

A CBS News article alleged to have established a connection between the CIA and Google.[302] "The investment arms of the CIA and Google are both backing a company that monitors the web in real time – and says it uses that information to predict the future."[303] The company—Recorded Future—allege they can provide real-time threat intelligence and "organize and analyze threat data in an entirely new and different way for better, faster security."[304] They also allege they can predict the future.[305]

The Brains Behind Google

Nafeez Ahmed does a nice job linking the CIA to Google from the beginning in his two-part series—*How the CIA made Google*.[306] Ahmed is very thorough and provides lots of documentation to support his assertions. He explains the role of In-Q-tel, Navy Captain Richard O'Neill and the Highland Forum,[307] Dr. Rick Steinheiser, Dr. Bhavani Thuraisingham,[308] and many more people, universities, corporations, groups, and government organizations. In part 2, Nafeez Ahmed highlights the cautions and warnings of Pulitzer Prize-winning Seymour Hersh,[309] [310] and others.

For clarification in the text below, MITRE, as explained on their website, is "a not-for-profit organization, MITRE works in the public interest across federal, state and local governments, and industry and academia."[311] MITRE was founded in 1958 to coordinate all the various companies and workers involved with the Air Force's massive airspace computer system. Since their initial relationship with the Air Force, MITRE has continued providing services for various government agencies. Nellie Ohr testified to Congress in the Russiagate probe that she worked for MITRE.[312, 313] MITRE was associated with Open Source Works that was a contractor for Director for Intelligence.[314]

Of particular interest are several paragraphs in which Nafeez Ahmed links Dr. Thuraisingham to the CIA and Sergey Brin:

> Thuraisingham was chief scientist for data and information management at MITRE, where she led team research and development efforts for the NSA, CIA...joint CIA-NSA program partly funded Sergey Brin to develop the core of Google, through a grant to Stanford managed by Brin's supervisor Prof. Jeffrey D. Ullman.

> Later, Dr. Thuraisingham posted a correction.[315] In her response, she also includes an information

sheet ("TITLE: Intelligence Community Initiative in Massive Digital Data Systems") at the end of Dr. Thuraisingham's correction links MITRE, NSA, DOD, and others in the Intelligence Community with efforts to manage large data sets.[316] In the Description section of the information sheet is a summary of the research efforts to develop *data management* technologies. These efforts paved the way for Google.

There are three very important things to note in her correction to Nafeez Ahmed's article *How the CIA made Google*.[317]

1. Dr. Thuraisingham does not dispute that the CIA, NSA, MITRE, and others in the intelligence community were fundamental to development of Google.

2. Dr. Thuraisingham only wanted to correct two small points:
   i. Dr. Thuraisingham retracted her assertion that Sergey Brin worked on the Flock Query System.
   ii. Dr. Thuraisingham challenged Nafeez Ahmed's assertion that the CIA **funded** Sergey Brin.[318]

3. Dr. Thuraisingham disputes nothing else except those two almost trivial details.

Who Funded Larry Page, Sergey Brin, and Professor Ullman

On page 6 of the 1977 Secretary of Defense Memorandum regarding mind control and behavior modification, "It appears that the Navy did act as a financial intermediary through which the Central Intelligence Agency dealt with an outside contractor that conducted one research effort that was part of the MKOFTEN project. It also appears that the Navy conducted, directly or through contractors, five programs in which Central Intelligence Agency sponsorship or participation and which resulted in the administration of drugs."[319]

Given what we can read from this memorandum regarding dopamine and mind-control research directed by the CIA but funded through US Navy, do you find it surprising that the CIA did not directly fund Dr. Ullman, Sergey Brin, and Larry Page? Instead of the money coming directly from the CIA, it appears the money came from (or through) the National Science Foundation.

- ✓ David Hart links Larry Page to National Science foundation.[320]
- ✓ Larry Page acknowledged support from NSF grant IRI-94-11306.[321]
- ✓ Sergey Brin acknowledged support from NSF grant IRI–96–31952.[322]

A National Science Foundation Grant (NSF Grant IRI-96-31952 Data Warehousing and Decision Support) was awarded to Jeffrey D. Ullman, Department of Computer Science, Stanford University[323] The grant was to support four students to design "database management systems that can handle complex queries involving the aggregation of very large amounts of data." The project was to begin on September 1, 1996, and end on August 31, 1999.

The group had previously been funded by another NSF grant (Award Number 9411306 for $4,516,573) beginning on September 16, 1994. This is the description of the project:[324]

> This project…is to develop the enabling technologies for a single, integrated and "universal" library, proving uniform access to the large number of emerging networked information sources and collections… The Integrated Digital Library is broadly defined to include everything from **personal information collections**, to the collections that one finds today in conventional libraries, to the large data collections shared by scientists. (Emphasis added.)

This grant was for supporting work "to develop the enabling technologies for a single, integrated, and "universal" library, proving uniform access to the large number of emerging networked information, sources, and collections. These include both online versions of preexisting works and new works and media of all kinds that will be available on the globally interlinked computer networks of the future."

In 2000, Professor Jeffrey D. Ullman, Department of Computer Science, Stanford University, provided an update on the impact of NSF Grant IRI-96-31952. "Google is a search engine company whose growth has brought it to the first rank, and that is growing faster than any of its competitors. This grant partially supported Google's core technology, which allows it to find pages far more accurately than other search engines."[325]

In spring and summer of 2019, the Department of Justice[326] and forty-nine state and the District of Columbia[327] were preparing potential investigates into Google for antitrust violations. Based on Dr. Ullman's comments—"This grant partially supported Google's core technology, which allows it to find pages far more accurately than other search engines."[328]—do you think that Google received an unfair market advantage? Should that be considered in the antitrust investigations?

The Government Technology and Services Coalition's Homeland Security Today (HSToday) posted an article on January 26, 2006 titled, *"While Fending Off DoJ Subpoena, Google Continues Longstanding Relationship With US Intelligence."*[329] The first part of the title before the comma is a moot point. The second part of the title is the most revealing, "Google Continues Longstanding Relationship With US Intelligence."

Do you think the last part of that title is an accurate summary of this chapter? In the next chapter, we will take a closer look at the CIA and some of their activities that shaped the situation we face today.

The CIA and MKULTRA

ollowing a two-year gap created by suddenly dissolving the OSS, the CIA got off to a bad start in 1947. The CIA was plagued with double agents and other agents that passed along disinformation from the enemy.[330] The CIA was desperate to regain control over a situation that eroded their effectiveness and credibility. Desperate situations can lead to desperate solutions. I make no apologies for what the CIA did or how they accomplished it. However, readers should evaluate the nefarious activities of the time against the existential threat the United States faced at the time.

Whether the existential threat was real or imaged is open for scrutiny. However, some of the methods used by the CIA to counter the existential threats were so horrific that they were hidden from the public for decades for fear of losing public support. Some in the CIA believed in the Machiavellian idea that the ends justified the means. The public disagreed and demanded better behavior and more accountability.

Nevertheless, what follows is an incredible account of one man with strong convictions who did not like what he saw. He died under mysterious circumstances. It took more than two decades, two Congressional hearings,[as] a presidential commission,[at] and a public

---

as   The first Congressional hearing was in 1975—United States Senate Select Committee to Study Governmental Operations with Respect to Intelligence Activities, 1975 Note: This is also known as the Church Committee after Senator Frank Church, who served as the chairperson of the committee. The second Congressional hearing was in 1977—Project MKULTRA, The CIA'S Program of Research in Behavioral Modification, Joint Hearing Before The Select Committee On Intelligence And The Subcommittee On Health And Scientific Research Of The Committee On Human Resources United States Senate Ninety-Fifth Congress, First Session, August 3, 1977.

at   United States President's Commission on CIA Activities within the United States. This is also called the Rockefeller Commission and was headed by Vice President Nelson Rockefeller.

apology by President Ford for the facts to overcome the narrative created by the Mighty Wurlitzer—or some reincarnation of the Mighty Wurlitzer.

Dr. Frank Olson

Dr. Frank Olson earned a PhD in bacteriology from the University of Wisconsin in 1938. He then served as a US Army officer stationed at Camp Detrick (now Fort Detrick) during World War II as one of the military officers working on biological warfare. After the war, he left the US Army. Nevertheless, he stayed on with the same program as a civilian researcher with the Army Biological Warfare Laboratories.

According to *The Guardian,* "Dr. Olson visited Porton Down, the UK's biological and chemical warfare research centre in Wiltshire, as well as bases in Paris, Norway, and West Germany. During these trips, according to the family's lawsuit, he 'witnessed extreme interrogations in which the CIA committed murder using biological agents that Dr Olson had developed.'"[331]

Many people were associated with Dr. Frank Olson in his ordeal. Lieutenant Colonel Vincent Ruwet was Dr. Frank Olson's immediate superior at the time of Frank's death. Dr. Robert V. Lashbrook received a PhD in chemistry and was a CIA chemist who worked with LSD. Dr. Lashbrook shared room 1018A at the Statler Hotel with Dr. Frank Olson the day Frank died.[332] Sid Gottlieb supervised most, if not all, the CIA mind-control research. He reported to Senior CIA Officer Richard Helms.[333] Richard Helms[au] oversaw much of the various MKULTRA programs and informed his boss, Allen Dulles,[av] that the research had to be conducted in "complete secrecy" so that the research would not jeopardize the reputation of top civilian scientists from universities and contractors around the country.[334] At the time of Dr. Olson's death, Richard Helms was the Deputy Director of Plans but would later become the Directory of the CIA. Helms believed that a foreign agent could not be trusted "unless you owned him body and

---

au   Later, Richard Helms would become director of CIA from June 30, 1966, until February 2, 1973.

av   Allen Dulles was the director of the CIA from August 23, 1951, until February 26, 1953.

soul." [sic] Helms believed mind-control programs would provide the tools to do just that.[335]

Time Lines

It is easy to get confused since there were many events, people, and organizations involved. Time lines may help keep track of things. This strange saga played over several years and involved many. By defining the time lines, it may be easier to see the cause and effect of what happened as well as the roles of various people involved. Later in this chapter, we will provide more details; however, it is probably best to start with just a brief outline of what happened and when.

1. On November 18, 1953, Dr. Frank Olson is covertly given LSD in his after-dinner drink.

2. Ten days later on November 28, 1953, Dr. Frank Olson dies under mysterious circumstances.

3. A presidential commission, led by Vice President Norman Rockefeller and hence the commission was nicknamed the Rockefeller Commission,[336] uncovers problems within the CIA. The commission began on January 4, 1975, and ended on June 6, 1975.

4. There were two Congressional hearings that looked into CIA activities. The first was the Senate Select Committee to Study Governmental Operations with Respect to Intelligence Activities (1975).[337]

5. On June 11, 1975, The *Washington Post* published a story about a civilian scientist falling out of the tenth-floor window of a hotel after he was given LSD without his knowledge by the CIA. The family realized the man in the *Washington Post* article was Dr. Frank Olson. His daughter—Lisa Olson Hayward—and her husband went to confront Ruwet, who had since retired. In an emotional meeting, Ruwet admitted what happened.[338] [339] Ruwet tried to convince the family not to go public with the information he did not have permission to tell them.[340] Instead, the Olson family went public.[341]

6. On July 10, 1975, the Olson family held a press conference seated at a table in their backyard.[342] Many members of the press attended. Dr. Frank Olson's wife and three adult children took turns reading a various part of a prepared statement.

    We feel our family has been violated by the CIA in two ways. First, Frank was experimented upon illegally and negligently. Second, the true nature of his death was concealed for twenty-two years … In telling our story, we are concerned that neither the personal pain this family has experienced nor the moral and political outrage we feel be slighted. Only in this way can Frank Olson's death become part of American memory and serve the purpose of political and ethical reform so urgently needed in our society.[343]

After the Olson family's press conference, things moved very quickly by Washington standards.

7. On July 21, 1975, President Ford invited the family to the White House for a formal apology.[344] [345] In the same year, the Senate passed Senate Resolution 21 that established

    [A] select committee of the Senate to conduct an investigation of Government intelligence activities, including the extent to which any illegal or improper activities were engaged in… Limits the expenses of such committee, under this resolution, to $750,000…. Restricts disclosure of information gathered by the committee, which would adversely affect intelligence activities of the CIA.[346]

8. The Olson family plea for political and ethical reform led to another Congressional hearing. On August 3, 1977 Congress began *A Joint Hearing Before The Select Committee On Intelligence And The Subcommittee On Health And Scientific Research Of The Committee On Human Resources United States Senate Ninety-Fifth Congress*.[347] These hearings exposed many more facts about Project MKULTRA and Dr. Olson's death.

9. These Congressional hearings also resulted in the Department of Defense admitting their part in the CIA's research. A few months later on September 20, 1977, the DoD release a memorandum cited earlier in this book—*Experimentation Programs Conducted by the Department of Defense That Had CIA Sponsorship or Participation and That Involved to Administration to Human Subjects Intended for Mind Control or Behavior-modification Purposes.*[348] *This document allows us to trace dopamine back to the CIA mind-control and behavior-modification programs.*

CIA's Institutional Mind-set at the Time

It is important to understand the CIA's institutional mind-set at the time Frank died. We can gain insights by reading several excerpts from the records of a Congressional hearing.[349]

While Richard Helms was deputy of Plans, he wrote,

While I share your uneasiness and distaste for any program which tends to intrude upon an individual's private and legal prerogatives, I believe it is necessary that the Agency maintain a central role in this activity, keep current on enemy capabilities the manipulation of human behavior, and maintain an offensive capability.[350]

A CIA inspector general wrote this astonishing statement,

Precautions must be taken not only to protect operations from exposure to enemy forces but also to conceal these activities from the American public in general. The knowledge that the Agency is engaging in unethical and illicit activities would have serious repercussions in political and diplomatic circles and would be detrimental to the accomplishment of its mission.[351]

Under these conditions, Dr. Frank Olson had a "moral crisis" and objected to CIA's "brain warfare."[352]

In 1953, Mr. Olson traveled to Europe and visited biological and chemical weapons research facilities. The Olson family lawsuit alleges that during that trip, Mr. Olson witnessed extreme interrogations, some resulting in deaths, in which the C.I.A. experimented with biological agents that he had helped develop.[353]

The CIA was concerned that Olson's "behavior was causing 'fear of a security violation.'"[354] According to the Congressional hearings, "On November 18, 1953, a group of ten scientists from the CIA and Camp Detrick attended a semi-annual review and analysis conference at a cabin located at Deep Creek Lake, Maryland."[355] After dinner, Sid Gottlieb spiked Frank Olson's after-dinner liqueur (Cointreau) with LSD that the CIA had been using for interrogation experiments. Apparently, Sid Gottlieb did not consider LSD harmful. After all, when he tried LSD himself, he woke up at five-thirty in the morning and milked his goats just as he did every other morning.[356]

LTC Ruwet decided Dr. Olson needed "psychiatric attention"[357] and what follows is a summary of relevant excerpts from the transcripts of the Congressional hearings. Ruwet called and told Lashbrook that Dr. Olson needed immediate professional attention. Lashbrook agreed to make the arrangements. Lashbrook, Ruwet and Olson flew to New York and meet with Dr. Harold Abramson. Dr. Abramson was not a psychiatrist but rather an allergist and immunologist practicing medicine in New York City. Abramson was associated with research supported indirectly by the CIA and was cleared by the CIA. Ruwet, Lashbrook, and Olson remained in New York for two days of consultations with Abramson. On Thursday, November 26, 1953, the three flew back to Washington so that Olson could spend Thanksgiving with his family. However, Olson told Ruwet that he was afraid to face his family. Olson and Lashbrook returned to New York while that Ruwet went to explain these events to Mrs. Olson. Lashbrook and Olson flew back to New York the same day for consultations with Abramson. Lashbrook and Olson spent Thanksgiving night in a Long Island hotel. On such short notice during the holiday travel season, Lashbrook and Olson could not get air transportation back to Washington for Friday. However, they were able to book a flight for Saturday morning. They checked into the Statler Hotel, had dinner, and two martinis each. Olson called the hotel operator and asked for a wakeup call and then when to bed. "According to Lashbrook, Olson was cheerful and appeared to enjoy the entertainment. He appeared no longer particularly depressed, and almost the Dr. Olson I knew prior to the experiment... At about 2:30 a.m. Saturday, November 28, Lashbrook was awakened by a loud crash of glass. In his report on the incident, he stated only that Olson had crashed through the closed window blind and the closed window and he fell to his death from the window of our room on the 10th floor."[358]

"We got a jumper!" shouted Jimmy—the door attendant at the Statler Hotel—"as he ran into the hotel lobby."[359] The CIA cover up began immediately[360] after Frank hit the sidewalk from falling out of a tenth-story window in the Statler Hotel in Long Island.[361] [aw] Again, summarizing from the transcripts of the Congressional hearings—Lashbrook immediately telephoned Gottlieb who in turn called Ruwett. Lashbrook then called the hotel desk to report the incident and after that he called Abramson. Abramson initially stated that "wanted to be kept out of the thing completely," but later changed his mind and agreed to assist Lashbrook.[362]

> In all my years in the hotel business," the night manager later reflected, "I never encountered a case where someone got up in the middle of the night, ran across a dark room in his underwear, avoiding two beds, and dove through a closed window with the shade and curtains drawn.[363]

A Lot of Emotional Pain for the Family but Dr. Frank Olson Did Not Die In Vain

He did not die in vain—however, all the events surrounding his death caused the Olson family a tremendous amount of emotional pain.

> Eric Olson says that his father's death and its aftermath had devastating consequences for his family. He said his mother, who is now dead, suffered from alcoholism. "We want justice," Mr. Olson said. "This has cost me an immense amount of time and years of my life."[364]

---

aw   Several sources say it was a thirteenth-story window. However, the Congressional testimony indicated it was the tenth-story window.

Both Lashbrook and Gottlieb attended the funeral of Dr. Frank Olson. Both men later asked to see Mrs. Alice Olson. She knew they did not work at Camp Detrick with Frank and was puzzled why they wanted to see her. LTC Ruwet told Alice it would make the two men feel better. According to Alice, "I did not want an ounce of flesh from them. I didn't think it was necessary, but, okay. I agreed. In retrospect it was so bizarre, it made me sick … I was a sucker for them."[365] "That visit unnerved her. Her coffee cup rattled in her hand… Years later Frank Olson's sons, Eric and Nils paid a visit to Sid Gottlieb who responded, "Oh my God, I'm so relieved to see you all don't have a gun."[366]

Without Frank Olson's tragic death and the audacity of the Olson family to call out the CIA, many secrets probably would have remained hidden. Few would have been able to link the current smartphone addiction back to the dopamine research conducted by the CIA. Few would have been able to link artificial intelligence back to CIA. Few would have been able to link the mind-control and behavior-modification research conducted by the CIA to a computer program that can "influence" people "towards a desired outcome."[367]

Now that we have established a link from early CIA research on mind control to the current problem of dopamine-mediated smartphone addiction, what else might we be able to learn? To find out what we might miss, we must carefully examine what happened and what were the official explanations.

Before he was the director of the CIA, Allen Welsh Dulles led CIA's research in mind control as a new method for interrogation[368] and behavior modification. CIA Director Allen Dulles had close relationships with wealthy and powerful patrons. These patrons also invested in MKULTRA mind-control research. Tom Baden, one of Allen Dulles top aides, provided these very wealthy and powerful patrons[ax] with semiannual briefings.[369] This begs several questions: Why were these wealthy and powerful patrons outside the CIA willing to invest in MKULTRA mind-control and behavior-modification research? What did these very wealthy and powerful patrons do with

---

ax   I deliberately left the names of these powerful and wealthy patrons out of this book in order to mitigate any allegations that I was trying to concoct a conspiracy theory. If you are interested in who these patrons were, check out the next reference.

the information they received from the semiannual briefings? If you can answer these questions, you may be able to understand why some things seem so weird these days. If I answered that question for you, I would immediately be labelled a conspiracy theorist. However, if I use the Socratic method of asking questions, you may be able to find the answer if you look hard enough and I will not be dismissed as a lunatic conspiracy theorist.

The DoD 1977 Memorandum

Shortly after Congress began investigating the CIA in their August 1977 hearings, [370] the Department of Defense admitted their part in the various CIA mind-control and behavior-modification programs. By this September 20, 1977, DoD memorandum,[371] we can trace dopamine research back to the Central Intelligence Agency,

> III. Navy Programs
>
> It appears from the available documents that the Navy was not involved in any aspect of the Central Intelligence Agency projects designated MKSEARCH and MKCHICKWIT. It appears that the Navy did act as a financial intermediary through which the Central Intelligence Agency dealt with an outside contractor that conducted one research effort that was a part of the MKOFTEN project. It also appears that the Navy conducted, directly or through contractors, five programs in which there was Central Intelligence Agency sponsorship or participation and which included the administration of drugs to human subjects for mind-control or behavior-modification purposes.

A brief explanation about the difference between DOPAMINE and DOPA may be helpful before reading the memorandum. Some lawsuits were dismissed and others resulted in fines. Dopamine is then used as a neurotransmitter. It is primarily active in the brain and less so in the nervous system outside the brain. Intravenous (IV) dopamine is sometimes used in critical care units to treat patients with low blood pressure.[372] Even if dopamine is given through IV or is ingested orally, it *does not pass* through the blood-brain barrier that serves to protect the brain. On the other hand, DOPA is a chemical compound that *can* pass through the blood-brain barrier. The brain converts dopa into dopamine.

Continuing on page 6, "In December, 1970, the contractor contacted the Central Intelligence Agency project officer directly and suggested research work on two types of drugs: analogs of **DOPA** and **dopamine**. (Emphasis added.)."

One page 7,[373] we read, "One of the research's progress reports shows an intention to publish the results of the first phase of this work, on analogs of DOPA and **dopamine**, at a professional meeting." (Emphasis added.)

Although the 1977 DoD memorandum answer some questions about the nexus between dopamine, the CIA, the DoD, the US Navy, civilian universities, and contractors, the DoD memorandum also raises some questions. What were the results from those taxpayers-funded studies on dopamine decades ago? Where are the reports? We do not know. Although, we may never know what was in the original dopamine research reports, today the connection between dopamine and smartphones addiction is obvious.

Allegedly, the documents associated with these projects and subprojects were destroyed. At least according to the testimony given to Congress, "The records of all these activities were destroyed in January 1973, at the instruction of then CIA Director Richard Helms."[374] Helms and other senior CIA officials destroyed almost all the documents in their possession of these programs because they feared a public backlash if what they did become widely known.[375]

Also, on page 9 of the Congressional report, "In brief, there were few records to begin with and less after the destruction of documents in 1973."[376]

We should parse those statements carefully. These statements may lead some to assume that *all* documents and data—at the CIA, universities, and contractors—were destroyed. The most important is what the statement does not explicitly state.

> In January 1973, MKULTRA records were destroyed
> by Technical Services Division personnel acting on the

verbal orders of Dr. Sidney Gottlieb, Chief of TSD. Dr. Gottlieb has testified, and former Director Helms has confirmed, that in ordering the records destroyed.[377]

It is important to note that only the records at the agency were destroyed. "[T]he bulk of the **agency's records** were destroyed in 1973."[378] (Emphasis added.) There is no indication that all the research records and data under the control of universities, contractors, and individuals outside the CIA also were destroyed. Nor is there any indication that someone within the CIA verified that all MKULTRA records outside the CIA were destroyed. The testimony to Congress did not say that all records and data that the universities and contractors had in their possession were also destroyed. It is unlikely the contractors and universities would destroy the information and data they gained from research.

Apparently, many MKULTRA mind-control and behavior-modification documents were saved from the alleged destruction. Decades later, an inventor would patent a method (8,095,492) that could use a computer to "influence" people "towards a desired outcome."[379] Who gets to determine the "desired outcome?" That is not stated in this patent. This patent infers that someone using the patented techniques can choose a wide range of possible outcomes for others without the targeted individual's consent.

Does that sound creepy? The word *covert* is used twice in this patent. If you have trouble accepting that idea, I urge you to read the patent yourself and form your own opinion. *MKULTRA* was used five times in this patent, and *artificial intelligence* was used once in this patent.[380] US Patent 8,095,492 states that a "list of documents related to MKULTRA can be found over the Internet." The inventor of the patent *does not disclose where* on the MKULTRA documents can still be found on the internet. This is a very notable oddity. In searching through hundreds of patents, I have never seen another case in which the US Patent Office allows information to be cited in a patent *without clearly indicating where others could find that information.*

In *The Bourne Legacy* movie, when their activities come under scrutiny from Congress, they said they would shut the program down. Consider the comments made by the fictional character retired Colonel

Eric Byer[ay] of *The Bourne Legacy*, "We won't lose it all. We've got the science. We'll keep the data ... Take a pause, and we'll rebuild it."

If you substitute Project MKULTRA instead of an engineered virus to alter behavior and control minds in *Jason Bourne* movies, then the movies appear less like science fiction and more like what the CIA did with MKULTRA mind-control and behavior-modification programs. We will examine more parallel themes between MKULTRA and Jason Bourne in another chapter. We will also investigate a patent that can covertly influence people to a "desired outcome" in more details in another chapter.

An Umbrella Project

MKULTRA was an umbrella project[381] under which the CIA funded certain sensitive subprograms.[382] At one point, the MKULTRA involved 86 universities or other civilian organizations.[383] In all, there were 149 subprograms arranged under these various MKULTRA projects.[384] Congressional hearings in 1977[385] provided more insights into the various projects. Information about the various MKULTRA projects and subprojects varies widely among different sources. Therefore, the "substantial quotations" below are direct quotations from the Congressional hearings.

> Project CHATTER was a Navy program that began in the fall of 1947. Responding to reports of "amazing results" achieved by the Soviets in using "truth drugs," the program focused on the identification and testing of such drugs for use in interrogations and in the recruitment of agents... The project expanded substantially during the Korean War, and ended shortly after the war, in 1953.
>
> Project BLUEBIRD/ARTICHOKE The earliest of the CIA's major programs involving the use of chemical and biological agents, Project BLUEBIRD, was approved by the Director in 1950. ... In August 1951, the project was renamed ARTICHOKE.

---

ay   The comments are at about the fourteen-minute and twenty-four-second mark.

MKNAOMI was another major CIA program in this area. In 1967, the CIA summarized the purposes of MKNAOMI... To stockpile severely incapacitating and lethal materials... To maintain in operational readiness special and unique items for the dissemination of biological and chemical materials... MKNAOMI was terminated in 1970.

MKULTRA was the principal CIA program involving the research and development of chemical and biological agents. It was "concerned with the research and development of chemical, biological, and radiological materials capable of employment in clandestine operations to control human behavior." In January 1973, MKULTRA records were destroyed.

MKULTRA began with a proposal from the Assistant Deputy Director for Plans, Richard Helms... outlining a special mechanism for highly sensitive CIA research and development projects that studied the use of biological and chemical materials in altering human behavior.

The inspector general's survey of MKULTRA in 1963 noted the following reasons for this sensitivity:

a. Research in the manipulation of human behavior is considered by many authorities in medicine and related fields to be professionally unethical; therefore, the reputation of professional participants in the MIKULTRA program are on occasion in jeopardy.

b. Some MKULTRA activities raise questions of legality implicit in the original charter.

c. A final phase of the testing of MKULTRA products places the rights and interests of US citizens in jeopardy.

d. Public disclosure of some aspects of MKULTRA activity could induce serious adverse reaction in

U.S. public opinion, as well as stimulate offensive and defensive action in this field on the part of foreign intelligence services.

Over the ten-year life of the program, many "additional avenues to the control of human behavior" were designated as appropriate for investigation under the MKULTRA charter. These include "radiation, electroshock, various fields of psychology, psychiatry, sociology, and anthropology, graphology, harassment substances, and paramilitary devices and materials.

The research and development of materials was conducted through standing arrangements with specialists in universities, pharmaceutical houses, hospitals, state and federal institutions, and private research organizations.

The next phase of the MKULTRA program involved physicians, toxicologists, and other specialists in mental, narcotics, and general hospitals, and in prisons ... conducted intensive tests on human subjects ... The Lexington Rehabilitation Center, as it was then called, was a prison for drug addicts serving sentences for drug violations ... As a reward for participation in the program, the addicts were provided with the drugs of their addiction.

LSD was administered to more than one thousand American soldiers who volunteered to be subjects in chemical warfare experiments.

For "Projects THIRDCHANCE and DERBY HAT, sixteen unwitting nonvolunteer subjects were interrogated after receiving LSD as part of operational field tests.

Which CIA Programs Were Stopped and Which Were Not?

A close examination of the list of 149 subprograms[386] and official statements offer some curious conclusions. The CIA director, Admiral

Stanfield Turner, offered some very carefully crafted statements. Many have interpreted the statements that the CIA completely shut down all mind-control and behavior-modification programs. Consider his statement: "Let me emphasize again that the MKUTRA events are 12 to 24 year in the past, and I assure you that the CIA is in no way engaged in either witting or unwitting testing of drugs today."[387]

There were 149 subprograms related to mind control and modification of human behavior.[388] By the time of the Congressional joint hearing, the CIA had already likely determined which drugs worked and which ones did not, so to continue researching drugs was no longer needed. Only a few of the 149 subprograms involved drugs. Below is a list of some subprograms that probably did not use drugs:

- 4, 15, and 19—investigations designed to utilize the art of deception for clandestine purposes
- 5, 29, and 49—hypnosis
- 43—a study of disassociated states
- 48—exploiting operational lines. Scientific methods and knowledge that can be utilized in altering attitudes, beliefs, thought processes, and behavior patterns of agent personnel
- 51—brain studies
- 67—**operational aspects of sex** (Emphasis added.)
- 120—operant conditioning in mice
- 134—psychological studies
- 141—program to obtain a feasible and practicable capability to **influence and control human behavior** (Emphasis added.)
- 142—**electrical brain stimulation** involving some new approaches (Emphasis added.)

Do you believe that all the nondrug subprograms were stopped? Is it possible that the research was continued by universities, contractors, or other civilian organizations? Consider two examples:

- Is *141—program to obtain a feasible and practicable capability to influence and control human behavior*—related to US Patent 8,095,492? This patent was issued decades later that patents a process that alleges the ability to covertly influence people to a "desired outcome." This will be covered in more details in another chapter—*Will Computers Be Able to ~~Brainwash~~ Influence People to a Desired Outcome?*

• Are other programs researching sex (program 67) and electrical brain stimulation (program 142) linked to several patents? You can decide for yourself after you read the next chapter.

Electronic, Magnetic, and Acoustic Viagra

The idea of tinfoil hats started in 1909.[389] In one of the most common connotations, a paranoid simpleton wears a tinfoil hat to protect their brain from electromagnetic fields, which might lead to mind control.

Common comedian parodies aside, it appears that someone—(or some group)—spent a tremendous amount of money, time, and effort researching and developing devices that can manipulate the nervous system by various methods. Consider some statements in a group of patents awarded to the same inventor. (The US patent numbers and *titles* are inside the parenthesis.):

> The invention can be used by the general public for inducing relaxation, sleep, or sexual excitement. (6,091,994—*pulsative manipulation of nervous systems*)[390]

> The method can be used by the general public ... for facilitation of relaxation and sexual arousal ... For both types of manipulation, the required subliminal subaudio acoustic pulses may be induced at one or both of the subject's ears by earphones. (6,017,302—*subliminal acoustic manipulation of nervous systems*)[391]

> With the same setup...a man 70 years of age can experience rather intense sexual excitement lasting for about an hour...sexual arousal has been observed. In a male subject 67 years of age the incidence of morning erections increased considerably. (6,081,744—*electric fringe field generator for manipulating nervous systems*)[392]

The setup…has been employed in the insomnia therapy experiments and the sexual arousal experiments discussed…sexual excitement sets in about one hour later. (6,238,333—*remote magnetic manipulation of nervous systems*)[393]

Certain devices based on this discovery may be used by the general public as a sleeping aid, or as an aid for relaxation, control of anxiety and stage fright, or for facilitation of sexual arousal. (5,800,481—*thermal excitation of sensory resonances*)[394]

The electric field was arranged to provide "a direct electrical driving of the brain. (6,506,148—*nervous system manipulation by electromagnetic fields from monitors*)[395]

It is yet a further object of the present invention to manipulate the nervous system by external electric fields, using low voltages that are generated by small and safe battery-powered devices with low current consumption. (6,167,304—*pulse variability in electric field manipulation of nervous systems*)[396]

The process of manipulating the nervous system is not only possible, but in some cases, it is remarkably easy. Furthermore, it does not take much energy. "The effectiveness of weak fields allows the use of **small battery-powered electric field generator**s that can be used conveniently by the general public as an aid to relaxation, sleep, or sexual excitement, and clinically for control and perhaps treatment of tremors and seizures, and disorders of the autonomic nervous system such as panic attacks"[397] (Emphasis added.)

If the nervous system can be manipulated by an electromagnetic field and it is possible "to manipulate the nervous system by external electric fields, using low voltages that are generated by small and safe battery-powered devices with low current consumption,"[398] then how long will it take until someone hacks smartphones and turns them into electronic Viagra? Maybe someone already has.

Ten of the fifteen patents from one inventor are for manipulating the brain, nervous system, or sensory system. (All fifteen patents from this one inventor can be seen in the endnotes.)[399] None of these ten patents shows a funding source or any association with a business, group, or government agency. No co-inventors were listed, which is unusual for patents like these that required a tremendous amount of research. (Bold emphasis added below.)

6,506,148 Nervous system **manipulation** by electromagnetic fields from monitors

6,238,333 Remote magnetic **manipulation** of nervous systems

6,167,304 Pulse variability in electric field **manipulation** of nervous systems

6,091,994 Pulsative **manipulation** of nervous systems

6,081,744 Electric fringe field generator for **manipulating** nervous systems

6,017,302 Subliminal acoustic **manipulation** of nervous systems

5,935,054 **Magnetic excitation** of sensory resonances

5,899,922 **Manipulation** of nervous systems by electric fields

5,800,481 **Thermal excitation** of sensory resonances

5,782,874 Method and apparatus for **manipulating** nervous systems

One has a choice of an acoustic, a magnetic, or an electromagnetic aphrodisiac. Several of these patents can be used for covert subliminal manipulation. One even includes a warning.

[E]lectromagnetic field pulses that excite a sensory resonance ... are so weak as to be subliminal. This is unfortunate since it opens a way for **mischievous application** of the invention, whereby people are exposed unknowingly to manipulation of their nervous systems for someone else's purposes. **Such application would be unethical and is, of course, not advocated**. It is mentioned here in order to alert the public to the possibility of **covert abuse** that may occur while being online or while watching TV, a video, or a DVD. (Bold emphasis added.)

Whom do you believe? Do you believe a noisy gaggle of comedian and talk show hosts that cutely belittle others as tinfoil hat conspirator theorists? Alternatively, do you believe the inventor that warned in an official US government document about potential covert abuse of this technology?

Another one of the patents provides more details. (6,506,148—Nervous system manipulation by electromagnetic fields from monitors)[400]

It is therefore possible to manipulate the nervous system of a subject by pulsing images displayed on a nearby computer monitor or TV set. For the latter, the image pulsing may be imbedded in the program material, or it may be overlaid by modulating a video stream, either as an RF signal or as a video signal. The image displayed on a computer monitor may be pulsed effectively by a simple computer program. For certain monitors, pulsed electromagnetic fields capable of exciting sensory resonances in nearby subjects may be generated even as the displayed images are pulsed with **subliminal** intensity. (**Bold**/emphasis added.)

Manipulating the Nervous System

How easy is it to manipulate the brain or nervous system?

For a TV monitor, the image pulsing may be inherent in the video stream as it flows from the video source, or else the stream may be modulated such as to overlay the pulsing. In the first case, a live TV broadcast can be arranged to have the feature imbedded simply by slightly pulsing the illumination of the scene that is being broadcast. This method can of course also be used in making movies and recording video tapes and DVDs.

Video tapes can be edited such as to overlay the pulsing by means of modulating hardware. A simple modulator is discussed wherein the luminance signal of composite video is pulsed... The same effect may be introduced at the consumer end, by modulating the video stream that is produced by the video source.[401]

Although the image below shows an old-style CRT monitor, the ability to manipulate the brain probably works with flat screen LCD displays. "Both LED and LCD TVs are based around LCD technology."[402] Therefore, in the following statement from patent 6,506,148, you can substitute LED or OED for LCD display. Reading from a patent, "Screen emissions also occur for liquid crystal displays (LCD). The pulsed electric fields may have considerable amplitude for LCD." Do you think large LED or OED flat screen could be hacked and, in turn, manipulate the nervous system of those nearby? Do you think smartphones with LED or OED and ear buds could be hacked and, in turn, manipulate the user's nervous system? These patents indicate that these scenarios are possible, but you can decide for yourself whether someone would actually try to hack your nervous system.

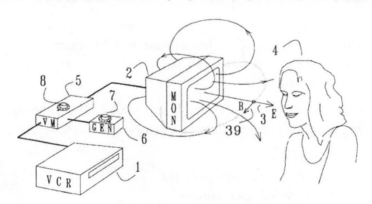

Figure 1 of Page 2

US Patent 6,506,148 Nervous system manipulation
by electromagnetic fields from monitors

> This is a work of the U.S. Government and is not
> subject to copyright protection in the United States.
> Foreign copyrights may apply.

According to the patent, it needs very little electric field to manipulate the brain. It seems this inventor has figured out how to manipulate the nerves going into the brain to do the heavy lifting.

> Certain cutaneous receptors may then be stimulated and they would provide a signal input into the brain along the natural pathways of afferent nerves. It has been found that, indeed, physiological effects can be induced in this manner by very weak electric fields.[403]

Here are more statements that are unusual. (6,238,333—*remote magnetic manipulation of nervous systems*)[404]

> [I]t possible to effectively manipulate the nervous system of a subject over a distance of several hundred meters, using a small portable battery-powered device.

> This makes it possible to manipulate a subject's nervous system over a range of several hundred meters, such as to cause relaxation and drowsiness.

> For military applications the device ... properly designed for compactness and for withstanding shock, can be air dropped or shot by mortar to locations near foes so that the latter can be subjected to magnetic manipulation

Were these patents the result of MKULTRA subprograms? Recalling from the previous chapter are some of the subprograms.

- 51—brain studies
- 67—operational aspects of sex
- 134—psychological studies
- 141—program to obtain a feasible and practicable capability to influence and control human behavior

You can decide for yourself whether you think these patents are associated with MKULTRA. Can you think of anyone or any group other than the CIA that would spend the time and money to develop methods to "effectively manipulate the nervous system of a subject over a distance of several hundred meters?"[405]

Many patents have a company listed in addition to the inventor's name. In contrast, these above-mentioned patents do not. Reading all fifteen patents, one can quickly understand that this one inventor spent a lot of time and effort in research to develop these inventions. Did this inventor do all the research and development from his own resources? We cannot know for sure.

This inventor has several other patents. The other patents also show a tremendous amount of research, and development was needed. Of note, one patent was for artificial intelligence 5,995,954, Method and apparatus for associative memory that was awarded on November 30, 1999. The inventor had acknowledged government funding for the research of this patent as well as for the several other patents but not for those patents that manipulate the brain or nervous system.

Nevertheless, we can see that one patent funded by DARPA[406] was for artificial intelligence (5,995,954 Method and apparatus for associative memory).[407] Four other patents states, "This invention was made prior to and during the course of work performed under a contract with the Office of Naval Research."[408]

Where else have we seen a Navy-funded research?

The next chapter takes an old profound historical injustice and translates it into modern terms courtesy of new technologies.

Mental Slavery

"Emancipate yourself from mental slavery"—this quote is attributed to Bob Marley (1945–1981), a Jamaican singer, songwriter, and a pioneer of reggae. He was ahead of his time in his understanding of how mental slavery would later affect millions—and maybe even billions—around the world.

In his book, *Hacking the American Mind*, bestselling author Robert Lusting, MD included a chapter titled, "Slaves to the Machine: How Did We Get Hacked?" In which he connects dopamine to mental slavery. Perhaps, we should explore that concept in more details.

Do you think it would be OK to covertly use psychological manipulation and deception on someone to influence them to do what you want? What if ideas were covertly planted into peoples' minds below the conscious level? Suppose the ideas would be so counter to people's normal thoughts and behaviors that they would immediately reject the ideas if those were recognized by their conscious mind, or suppose the ideas are not rejected because they are not recognized by the conscious mind since the implanted ideas were planted in the mind "below the conscious level." Those "influencing actions" would have significant influence on decisions. You may think that is far-fetched. Unfortunately, it is not. It is already a patented process—US Patent 8,095,492.[409]

Suppose that someone would use the process described in US Patent 8,095,492 to modify someone's behavior. *Physical* slavery is illegal and morally reprehensible. If a depraved character is covertly able to turn others into *mental* slaves, how might they use the *mental slaves*?

- Mental slaves could be used to create echo chambers to advance political or social narratives.

- Mental slaves could be influenced to vote contrary to how they would have voted had they not been brainwashed. Consider the effect mental slaves may have on a close election. They could tip elections for or against particular ballot measures or candidates. Mental slaves could greatly pose a serious threat to democracy.

- Mental slaves could promote new fads and merchandize, guaranteeing huge profits for those selling the goods and services.

- Mental slaves could be brainwashed to buy goods and services until they are broke as a joke.

Recall comments earlier in this book from former Google Product Manager Tristan Harris, who stated, "They are shaping the thoughts and feelings and actions of people. They are programming people"[410] If you thought Tristan Harris was exaggerating, you may want to reconsider.

It might tempt you to ask a question. Why isn't mental slavery illegal just like physical slavery? It should be, but it is not. I could not find any laws or regulations that specifically addressed mental slavery. U.S. Code, Title 18. Crimes And Criminal Procedure, Part I. Crimes, Chapter 77. Peonage, Slavery, And Trafficking In Persons Sections 15811597[411] only addresses slavery in the physical sense.

Perhaps, it is because it is more subtle and harder to define mental slavery than physical slavery. Nevertheless, it is still slavery.

Physical slavery enabled New Orleans Louisiana to become the wealthiest city[412] in the United States in 1840. Will Silicon Valley become New Orleans 2.0? Rephrasing that slightly, will Silicon Valley become the internet version of New Orleans, where wealth is generated not by *physical* slavery but by *mental* slavery facilitated by computer-aided mind control programs?

Have some unsuspecting people been sucked in by an invisible electronic vortex into *mental* slavery without realizing their minds have been hacked and are being remotely controlled? Have some been sucked into something like *The Matrix* with realizing their fate?

Electronic Parasitism and High-Tech Parasites

The National Geographic has an article that explains how some parasites can hack the brains and control the behavior of the parasites' hosts. In one example, hairworms hack and control the brains of crickets so crickets commit suicide and drown themselves in water. Then the hairworms swim away in the water. There are more creepy examples.[413]

Merriam Webster offers several definitions that may be helpful for understanding high-tech parasites.

✓ Definition of *parasitism*: the behavior of a parasite.[az]

✓ Definition of *symbiosis:* a cooperative relationship (as between two persons or groups)

Tech companies and tech billionaires would like you to think their relationship with you is symbiotic instead of parasitic. If a ~~propaganda~~ public relations campaign is successful, many people would probably believe and vigorously defend a narrative instead of the facts. If you want to know what the facts are, ask yourself some questions:

• Who lives like rock stars? Who lives by modest means?

• Who flaunts their wealth by traveling around the world in private jets and luxury yachts? Who would like to travel the world but cannot afford to? Who walks or travels by bicycle, public transportation, Uber, or Lyft?

---

az   Definition of *parasite*: something that resembles a biological parasite in dependence on something else for existence or support without making a useful or adequate return.

- Who lives in expensive mansions? Who lives in modest dwellings?

- Who owns a large tract of land in Hawaii and other nice places? Who would be delighted to have a half-acre for a garden?

- Who grew amazingly wealthy while you paid the bills?

After you answer those questions, do you think your relationship with tech companies and tech billionaires leans toward being symbiotic or parasitic?[ba] The next paragraph gets more graphic. You might want to skip the next paragraph if you do not like to think yucky thoughts.

In an abstract equivalency, there may be an *electronic equivalent of wormy parasites*. The bad news is that if your brain has been *covertly infested with electronic parasites that have wormed their way into your brain, those electronic parasites may have trashed your brain*.

The good news is that your brain has a tremendous ability to heal itself.[414] *If your brain has been infested by high-tech parasites and trashed, you can be made whole again.* The last chapter has many suggestions that can help you.

---

ba   Please note that is not meant to be hate speech. Instead, it is meant to be an intellectual exercise in comparisons based on verifiable scientific facts and legal definitions.

Will Computers Be Able to ~~Brainwash~~ Influence People to Desired Outcomes?

emember MKULTRA subprogram 141? This was the program designed "to obtain a feasible and practicable capability to **influence and control human behavior**." (Emphasis added.)

Recall comments earlier in this book from former Google Product Manager Tristan Harris, who stated, "They are shaping the thoughts and feelings and actions of people. They are programming people" [415] Do you think there is any similarity of Tristan's comment to the goals of MKULTRA subprogram 141? Do you think US Patent 8,095,492[416] might be related to MKULTRA subprogram 141?

Yes, because this patent uses *MKULTRA* five times in the patent. This patent alleges a computer system can automatically recommend "influence actions" that can "influence" people "towards a desired outcome."[417] [bb] This may be the most important question in this book for you to try to answer. Alternatively, if you choose to take a blue pill, this next question may be the most important question in your life.

---

bb   "A computer system that is operable for automatically recommending influence actions to a user comprising: a processor; an interface for receiving situation data regarding a situation and a desired outcome".

Who gets to determine what is the "desired outcome" for you?

This patented process enables a computer to custom-design a brainwashing program for a specific individual based on their unique experiences and characteristics. "Artificial Intelligence" (P. Winston, Addison-Wesley, 1992)[418] was also referenced in this patent.[419]

Not only does the inventor of this patent reference MKULTRA as a source of information but also several other sources on how to con or manipulate people. The inventor provides an "overview of social research regarding influence" in this patent. The inventor cites several experts who have done in-depth analysis on how to con, fool, deceive, trick, and exploit vulnerabilities in people. Here is a summary of some cited experts and their intellectual contributions[bc] to this patent: (**Bold/** emphasis added in multiple places below.)

> Chuck Whitlock has done extensive work identifying and demonstrating **deceptive influences**. His book[bd] includes detailed descriptions and examples of many common **street deceptions**. Fay Faron[be] points out that most such confidence efforts are carried out as specific `plays` and details the anatomy of a 'con'
>
> Bob Fellows[bf] examines how 'magic' and similar techniques **exploit human fallibility** and cognitive limits **to deceive people**. According to Bob Fellows... the following characteristics **improve the chances of being fooled**. (You can read in the patent about the sixteen methods to deceive people.)
>
> Fellows also identify a set of methods used to manipulate people. **The illusion of free choice** is an

---

bc   There is no evidence that the name individuals knowingly cooperated with the inventor of this patent. Nevertheless, their intellectual efforts were utilized by the inventor of this patent. Therefore, their intellectual contributions were involuntary and unwittingly.

bd   Chuck Whitlock "Scam School," MacMillan, 1997

be   Fay Faron, "Rip-Off: A Writer's Guide to Crimes of Deception," *Writers Digest Books*, 1998, Cinn, Ohio.

bf   Bob Fellows, "Easily Fooled," *Mind Matters*, PO Box 16557, Minneapolis, Minn. 55416, 2000.

example where the victim has choice but no matter what choice is made, as long as it fits the constraints of the person carrying out the deception, the victim will appear to have had their mind read. This is an example of a posteriori proof. The deception involves a different path to the desired solution depending on the solution required by the 'free choice' of the victim. Mind control is exerted through social influence that restricts freedom of choice. It consists of **psychological manipulation, deception, and the use of 'demand characteristics'**

Thomas Gilovich[bg] "provides in-depth analysis of human reasoning fallibility by presenting evidence from psychological studies that **demonstrate a number of human reasoning mechanisms resulting in erroneous conclusions.**

Charles K. West[bh] "describes the steps in psychological and social distortion of information and provides detailed support for **cognitive limits leading to deception**.

The computer program can continuously track the progress of "influencing" and automatically adjust the "influencing actions" until the **person is finally ~~programmed~~ influenced to the "desired outcome."** This is how the inventor explains the process in the patent:

> Tracking Progress…the invention involves methods and/or systems and/or modules that provide a way to track status and/or progress over time to guide, instruct, or otherwise assist individuals or groups about how to influence other individuals or groups in order to achieve objectives.

In other words, "individuals or groups" can use robot **computers to ~~program~~ influence human behavior**.

---

bg   Thomas Gilovich, "How We Know What Isn't So: The Fallibility of Human Reason in Everyday Life," Free Press, NY, 1991.

bh   Charles K. West, "The Social and Psychological Distortion of Information," Nelson-Hall, Chicago, 1981.

Consider some of the words and short phrases used in US Patent 8,095,492 and its patent application.[420]

> [A]rtificial intelligence ... brainwash ... CIA's "manual on trickery" ... con ... covert ... creating deceptive statistics ... deceive ... deceptions ... deceptive influences ... desired outcome ... distorts facts in favor of 'flavor' ... employing hidden information ... exploit human fallibility ... exploitation ... false consensus effect ... inspire fear and insecurity ... manipulation ... mind control ... MKUTRA ... power and influence ... predetermined ... strategies and tactics ... subliminal persuasion ... threats.

Consider some comments contained in this patent:

> [M]uch of the effect of influence techniques is built-in below the conscious level of most people .... exploitation by professionals for gaining compliance to desired behaviors ... a substantial series of psychological experiments that demonstrate quite clearly how people react to situations without a high level of reasoning ... promote illogical thinking and impulsiveness to the point where the recipient would be discredited in public ... Keep people off balance and in the dark by never revealing the purpose behind your actions ... Use mystery to beguile, seduce, even frighten ... Ask indirect questions to get people to reveal their weaknesses and intentions ... You become the master of others ... Play a sucker. No one likes feeling stupider than the next person. The trick, then, is to make your victims ... feel smart - and not just smart, but smarter than you are. Once convinced of this, they will sucker - never suspect that you may have ulterior motives ... People have an overwhelming desire to believe in something. Become the focal point of people's need such desire by offering them a cause, a new faith to follow. Keep your words vague but full to believe to of promise; emphasize enthusiasm over rationality and

clear thinking ... Teach no one your tricks or they will be used against you ... The best deceptions are the ones that seem to give the other person a choice ... The truth is often avoided because it is ugly and unpleasant ... There is great power in tapping into the fantasies of the masses ... You must seduce others hearts and into wanting to move in your direction. A person you have seduced becomes your loyal minds of pawn. And the way to seduce others is to operate on their individual psychologies and other's weaknesses. Soften up the resistant by working on their emotions, playing on what they hold dear and what they fear.

How do you feel now that you know a computer program can use "influencing actions" like those mentioned above to play people like suckers? Who would use this and why? This computer system allegedly can analyze a person's unique attributes, characteristics, and experiences and provide a "power produces influence" chart made as to which forms of overt, *covert*, and bridging influence are available to be applied.

Yes, you read that correctly. *Covert* means without a person's knowledge. This patent alleges that the computer system described in this patent can covertly influence a person. That means against their will. Is that legal?

Criticism and Commentary

This patent contains many individual words and phrases dispersed throughout that indicate an intention to manipulate people covertly without their awareness or consent. "Substantial quotation"[bi] from this patent is necessary because it is a multitude of statements that support the allegation that this patented process can manipulate people covertly without their awareness or consent. Because the inventor cites research

---

bi   "Substantial quotations" are necessary because the plethora of material in this text that indicates an intent to manipulate people without their consent. Without directly quoting the material for criticism and commentary, it would be easy to dismiss the author's criticism of this patent as conspiracy theory. Although many publishers have restricted guidelines of no more than four lines for fair use, several court cases have affirmed that "substantial quotation" is allowed in some circumstances. More information and discussion on fair use and copyrights are contained in an annex at the end of this book.

from MKULTRA, many people could make a reasonable extrapolation that "influence" as used in this patent can also mean brainwashing.

Do you think covert manipulation or brainwashing should be legal? Whether it is legal or not, it may also be almost irrelevant. If the financial return is large enough, it is likely that the corporation would hire a very large stable of high-priced lawyers to wear down litigants in court for years until they can no longer continue the costly legal marathon. After all, influencing people to buy products and services with advertisements is legal. Where does a judge or jury draw the line to define what is legal influencing and illegal brainwashing? High-priced lawyers can intentionally blur those distinctions.

Based on the information in this patent, here are some questions to ponder:

- ✓ Who gets to determine the "desired outcome"?
- ✓ Who gets to manipulate?
- ✓ Who gets to deceive?
- ✓ Who gets to exploit human fallibility?
- ✓ Who gets to brainwash others?
- ✓ Who gets to use the "manual on trickery"?
- ✓ Who creates deceptive statistics?
- ✓ Who gets to use deceptive influences?
- ✓ Who gets to use false consensus effects?
- ✓ Who gets to inspire fear and insecurity?
- ✓ Who gets to use subliminal persuasion?

How do all these fit together? This patent indicates that a computer program can be used with "games and entertainments." Do you think they might first try to get people addicted to "games and entertainments" on their smartphones and then covertly steer them toward a desired outcome?" Does "entertainment" include social media? Are individuals that frequently use social media on their smartphones vulnerable to being "influenced" toward a "desired outcome" that someone else has covertly choose for them? Have some people already been unwittingly pulled into something like *The Matrix* (1999) without realizing it?

US Patent 8,095,492 was filed on November 1, 2006. Since 2006, the population of the United States has become more polarized in culture, politics, religious views, identities, and other social dimensions. Do you think it is possible that at least a small portion of the polarization since 2006 could be the result of this patent? Do you think that maybe some of the polarization has been ~~programmed~~ influenced by some *Dr. Strangelove* types using this patented process? Admittedly, that is an absurd question. However, it is meant to draw attention to an important logical question. If an individual or group cannot change behaviors of others by merits of their ideas presented in open and public dialog, how can we trust those who would use a computer program that can covertly influence people at a subconscious level? This begs another question. Why was this program developed, and who are the individuals or groups that need to be covertly ~~brainwashed~~ influenced?

Next, let us explore the many parallels between MKULTRA and the *Jason Bourne* movie series.

Jason Bourne

The CIA has been involved in movies for a long time. The film version of *Animal Farm* was funded by the CIA in the 1950's.[421] In 2001, the CIA "appointed an official PR liaison with Hollywood: veteran CIA operative Chase Brandon…"[422] The CIA makes no secret about its involvement with the entertainment industry. The *CIA Entertainment Industry Liaison* even has a standing offer:[423]

> [I]f you are part of the entertainment industry, and are working on a project that deals with the CIA, the Agency may be able to help you. We are in a position to give greater authenticity to scripts, stories, and other products in development. That can mean answering questions, debunking myths, or arranging visits to the CIA to meet the people who know intelligence — its past, present, and future.

At the end of the *Jason Bourne* movies is the following statement:

> The characters and events depicted in this photoplay are fictitious. Any similarity to actual persons, living or dead, is purely coincidental.

If you read that statement quickly and do not analyze it carefully, it may appear to be an all-inclusive statement. By cleverly mentioning *events* in the first sentence but not the second sentence, this statement implies that any similarity to actual *events* is purely coincidental. Furthermore, if you read the statement carefully, it *does not state* the following:

> Any similarity to actual *programs, events, or themes* within the CIA is purely coincidental.

Therefore, let us examine some similarities to *programs, events, and themes* that might be intentional and not coincidental.

The *Jason Bourne* novels and movie series has a series of projects and programs with one leading to another and often overlapping.

- SILVERLAKE
- BLACKBRIAR
- TREADSTONE
- OUTCOME

There were 149 subprojects within the MKULTRA umbrella.[424] The subprojects were grouped into various "projects" that were made public by the 1977 Senate Committee on Intelligence hearings. (These are listed verbatim as they are written in the Congressional transcripts. Some projects are preceded by the word *project* and others are not.)[425]

1. Project CHATTER
2. Project BLUEBIRD/ARTICHOKE
3. MKNAOMI
4. MKULTRA
5. MKDELTA
6. MKSEARCH
7. OFTEN/CHICKWIT
8. Project THIRDCHANCE
9. Project DERBY HAT

A predominate theme in *Jason Bourne Identify* was amnesia. We see from the Congressional hearings that producing amnesia was one goal of Sub-Projects 35 and 54 of MKULTRA.[426] Subproject 61 was brain studies.[427] MKULTRA subproject 120 was operant conditioning.[428] Subproject 134 was psychological studies.[429]

MKULTRA subproject 48 was designed to altering attitudes, beliefs, thought processes, and behavioral patterns.[430] In comparison to the *Jason Bourne* series, altered attitudes, beliefs, thought processes, and behavioral patterns were attributed to a specially engineered virus. In *Jason Bourne Identity*[bj] Conklin uses the term *behavioral software* regarding how Jason Bourne was programmed. Moreover, Dr.

---

bj   The comment is at about the 1:07:30 time mark.

Marta Shearing makes a comment in *Bourne Legacy*[bk]—"And, people there are working on behavioral design. It's programmable behavior, neural design."

Could the comments about *behavioral software* and *behavioral design* be related to US Patent 8,095,492 that uses a computer system to ~~brainwash~~ "influence" people towards a "desired outcome"? If you recall, this patent contains the word *brainwashing* and cites research from the CIA's Project MKULTRA.

DARPA funded a patent (5,995,954)[431] for artificial intelligence[432] that relies on artificial electronic *neural networks* for learning. *Bourne Legacy* was released in **2012**. US Patent 5,995,954 was also awarded in **2012**.

Jason Bourne's sensory deprivation and deliberately inflicted "clinical" trauma appears to be similar to MKULTRA "psychic driving" by Dr. Donald Ewen Cameron, a Canadian psychiatrist. Cameron used several methods for "depatterning." These include isolating people in a sleep room for up to one hundred and one days, electroshock, insulin overdoses, and hallucinogens like LSD. After breaking them, Cameron attempted to reprogram them by playing recorded messages to them for most of the waking hours for several weeks. Author Naomi Klein wrote, "He was a genius at destroying people, but he could not remake them.[433] His methods were so barbaric that after Cameron's death, Canada settled out of court with Alison Steel the daughter of one of the victims, Jean Steel.[434] While conducting his "research," Cameron compared his patients to prisoners of war stating, *"[L]ike prisoners of the Communist, tended to resist [treatment] and had to be broken down."* Do you think Cameron's statement is similar to a statement by Ward Abbot in *Jason Bourne Supremacy*[bl]—"His mind is broken. We broke it."

At the end of *Jason Bourne Supremacy*, Pam Landy tells Jason that his real name is David Webb. In *Jason Bourne* (2016), we see his father's name is Richard Webb. David Webb's father, Richard, allows *Jason Bourne* (David Webb) to become ensnared in the CIA's behavior modification program. The treatment *Jason Bourne* (David Webb)

---

bk   The comment is at about the 58-minute and 20-second mark.

bl   The comment is at about the 59-minute and 20-second mark.

endured as portrayed in the movie is similar to the description of those notable horrific treatments many received in MKULTRA at the hands of Dr. Cameron, Dr. Wolff, and others.

Dr. Harold Wolff was trained by the famous Russian Ivan Pavlov[435] who received a Nobel Prize and was mentioned earlier in this book. Dr. Wolff was a friend and frequent dinner guest of Allen Dulles. Dr. Wolff received large grants for research and then steered millions to other researchers.[436] Allen Dulles's son, Allen Macy Dulles Jr., was wounded in the head by shrapnel from a mortar while serving with the Marines in the Korean War.[437] Allen Dulles turned his son over to Dr. Wolff for treatment. Allen Dulles's daughter, Joan, wrote of the horrible treatments her brother Sonny received from Dr. Wolff, including among other things, insulin shock therapy.[438] Later, Joan wrote something as poignant today as it was back then and should be remembered by all future generations regarding brain research—"Once you go to the dark side, there seems to be no limit."[439]

No Drugs But Is There Anything Else?

If you recall from an earlier chapter, Admiral Stansfield Turner testified at Congressional hearings on August 3, 1977, "and I can assure you that the CIA is in no way engaged in either witting or unwitting testing of **drugs** today."[440] (Emphasis added.)

However, he did not make the same categorically statement that all mind-control and behavioral-modification research was halted. Nor did he say that any of the MKULTRA subprojects that did not use drug were halted. Aside from these, he did not say that any of the other 149 subprograms that did not use drugs were halted. Therefore, is it possible that other subprojects continued (e.g., brain studies, hypnosis, behavioral modification, altering attitudes, beliefs, thought processes, and behavioral patterns; operant conditioning, etc.)?

As a matter of fact, Admiral Stanfield Turner testified that he was very deliberately trying not to indicate which of the MKULTTRA projects were still ongoing.

Admiral TURNER. Yes, sir. **I have not tried to indicate that we either are not doing or would not do**

any of the things that were involved in MKULTRA,
but when it comes to the witting or unwitting testing
of people with drugs, that is certainly verboten.[441]
(Emphasis added.)

Pamela Landy? → Gina Haspel?

Consider the character of Pamela Landy played many roles in the
Jason Bourne movie series including the deputy director of the CIA. In
the movie series, Pamela Landy realizes there are black hats within the
CIA and tries to thwart their efforts. *Mad Magazine* popularized the
concept of white-hat spies (good guys) and black-hat spies (bad guys).

I suspect that most people in the CIA today are white hats.
However, given the very powerful tools that their disposal, it would
only take a few black hats to go rouge and cause tremendous damage.
Are there enough white hats in the CIA now to rein in the black hats?

On February 5, 2019, during the State of the Union Address, Gina
Haspel, the current director of the CIA, was televised very briefly on
C-SPAN. The image of her was so quick that most people probably did
not notice the line drawings on her blouse. On first glance, it appeared
to be just a white blouse with many thin curved lines and a few small
splashes of color. On closer examination, it was unmistakable. The
whirls of thin lines and splashes of color were many women's white sun
hats with colorful ribbons hiding in plain sight.

Was Gina Haspel sending a subtle signal in plain sight that she
is a white hat and she intends to rein in the black hats? Alternatively,
is Gina Haspel part of the corrupt Deep State? Was the blouse with
white hats just a ruse or a clever disinformation campaign? History
will eventually reveal what is in her heart as well as her strength and
weaknesses. I really, really hope she is a white hat that she can clean
up a history of malfeasance. If not, we need to buckle up and hang on
tight because it will be a very rough ride.

What Can You Do?

Are you OK with being a mental slave, electronically parasitized, and exploited by others? If the answer is yes, then please ask yourself that question at least once a year—several times a year would be even better.

If you struggle with your smartphone, there is no shame in admitting you get temporary pleasure by getting squirts of dopamine—after all that is how your brain normally works. You should not feel any shame. They deceived you. They did not tell you that they would covertly use dopamine to manipulate the pleasure/reward pathway in your brain without your consent. Some cunning swindlers took advantage of your good nature. They told you they would provide you a pleasurable internet experience. That was a clever half-truth to mislead you. They took advantage of you and even betrayed your trust. They did not tell you the dopamine research was paid for by the CIA as part of mind-control and behavior-modification projects.

Some may have covertly and electronically wormed their way into your brain and trashed your brain. Now that you know, are you going to let them continue to get away with it? If they got you hooked on dopamine and it made you anxious, depressed, and lowered your patience threshold, what are you going to do about it?

If you are a smartphone addict, you should first admit that they addicted you. If it is too much for you to admit it to someone else, at least admit it to yourself. Are you going to do nothing about it, or are you going to fight back? Just because they may have trashed your brain does not mean your brain has to stay trashed—your brain has the ability to heal.[442] [443] [444] [445] However, you have to start the process.

If you are *not* a smartphone addict but you enjoy getting a few squirts of dopamine from time to time, you need to admit your dopamine dependency. You also need to realize that you may slowly slip into a being a dopamine addict without realizing it.

If you are not sure if you are a smartphone addict, you can take an online quiz.[446] As I mentioned earlier, it is based on self-reporting and may be subjective. However, if you are in doubt, it is a good place to start.

If none of the above applies to you, then you are fortunate that your genes did not predispose you to be vulnerable to addictions. Additionally, I hope this book has provided you with the insight into why others struggle with smartphone addiction.

Who Is Protecting the Little Children?

People would be enraged if a drug dealer sneaked into someone's home or a day care and gave little children cocaine. Yet there is no outrage when smartphones stimulate a dopamine release that stimulates the pleasure/reward pathway in the brain in a manner similar to cocaine.

Instead, many people use smartphones as an electronic babysitter or electronic nanny to pacify little children. Some even think it is cute. Is it cute, or is it dangerous?

For thousands of years we were ignorant of the damage lead could cause. However, now we now know that—

> Even low-level lead exposures in developing babies have been found to affect behavior and intelligence… Generally, lead affects children more than it does adults. Children tend to show signs of severe lead toxicity at lower levels than adults. [447]

American Academy of Pediatrics issued a policy statement with board guidelines. [448] However, these guidelines are very broad in comparison to exposure limits to lead and other toxic compounds. Currently, there is not enough scientific data to understand the risks to little children from smartphone addiction as there is for lead exposure.

If you recall from earlier in this book, allegedly Apple refused to sell Dopamine Lab's app to decrease dopamine addiction. Smartphones have facial recognition technology, voice recognition technology, precision geolocation technology, and artificial intelligence. Are high-tech companies and app developer quietly lobbying elected officials and regulators? Are they lobbying and discouraging funding for research that would provide more precise exposure limits to prevent smartphone addiction in little children?

Smartphones are *smart* enough to determine if smartphones are being used by little children or adults. Tech companies and app designers could have already designed apps that would prevent little children from becoming addicted to smartphones. However, they have not. Are high-tech companies already conditioning little children so they are so thoroughly addicted to smartphones that the tech billionaires will be wealthy mental slave masters and turn Silicon Valley into New Orleans 2.0?

If you want to help protect the little children, contact your elected officials and demand they fund the research needed to provide exposure limits that would help prevent little children from becoming addicted to smartphones. If you knew a drug dealer sneaked into a home or daycare and gave a little child cocaine, would you contact the police? Why wouldn't you contact your elected officials and demand they pass laws and regulations to protect the little children from becoming smartphone addicts before they can walk or talk?

Practical Solutions for Dopamine Addiction or Dependency

If you—or someone you know—has been caught in the dopamine trap, here are a few things that may help:

1. If they tricked you into becoming a mental slave—"Emancipate yourself from mental slavery" (Bob Marley).

2. Disable notifications and change display from color to gray scales.[449]

3. Get more dopamine from exercise [450] [451] and less from smartphones or video gaming. Transition slowly so you do not over exercise and cause athletic injuries.

4. Use an old-fashion, dumb cell phone whenever possible instead of a smartphone.

5. Robert Lustig, MD offers several suggestions that may help in his book *Hacking the American Mind*.[452]

6. August Brice offers ten suggestions that can help you dampen the dopamine urge.[453]

7. Take advantage of free online resources. There are many. This is just a small sample.
   - HelpGuide has many more tips that may help you overcome smartphone addiction.[454]
   - Treatment for Addiction to Smartphones[455]
   - Addicted to Your Smartphone? Here's What to Do[456]

8. The Royal Society for Public Health offers six suggestions that may help counter harmful effects of social media.[457]

9. Seek out a treatment program. These include both outpatient and inpatient programs.

10. Detox from your smartphone cold turkey. Post a note on your social media that you are detoxing cold turkey for a week and will not be responding to any posts. Get a cheap cell phone on a prepaid plan. Inform anyone that might need to contact you in an emergency and give them your new temporary number. Call your service provider and tell them they are part of your smartphone addiction, and you need them to suspend temporarily your service on your smartphone for one week. If they refuse, inform them that if you get into an accident because you were distracted due to your smartphone addiction, they will be subject to litigation under "proximate cause" and "substantial effect."[458] Services providers will incur more legal liability if you asked for their help and they refuse to help you overcome dopamine addiction that they helped create and even profited from your addiction.

11. Ask your elected officials to pass laws that force tech companies to offer for sale "time-out" apps similar to what Dopamine Labs allegedly tried to sale on Apple Store.[459]

12. For parents that may be concerned their children are addicted to smartphones, the National Institute of Drug Abuse (NIDA) also provides some excellent information

regarding "Principles of Substance Abuse Prevention for Early Childhood."[460] It explains some risk factors and strategies to prevent substance abuse. Even though this article is using the term "substance abuse," it also applies to smartphone addiction since substance abuse and smartphone addiction share the same neurotransmitter (dopamine). They also share the same reward/pleasure neuronal pathway in the brain.

13. HealthyChildren.org also offers many helpful suggestions to parents of young children.[461]

14. If you are concerned about addiction to video games, ask your elected officials to pass laws that would require video games to have time-outs and halftimes just like in athletic competitions. For example, the basketball half-time period lasts fifteen minutes for both college and NBA games, Why not the same for video games? Sitting in one place for a long time can cause so-called Gamer's Thrombosis.[462] Several news organizations raised awareness of the problem in 2013. A fatality was recorded in 2016.[463] Because of the competitive market for video games, it is unlikely that any video games programmers will unilaterally impose time-outs and halftimes. Remember, this is a dopamine-enabled addiction.

Work Together and Help Each Other

We need to help each other. Tell your family and friends. Educate your friends. Share what you have learned from this book with them. Contact your elected officials. Tell the tech companies what you will not accept any longer.

Peer pressure can be a good thing. If your friends were too drunk or high on drugs to drive, ride a bicycle, and stumble around by themselves, would you tell them? Friends help friends. If you want to have friends, you need to be a friend. You would surely warn a friend if they were not paying attention and likely to fall off a cliff. Will you be at peace with yourself if you do nothing as you watch your friends get sucked into dopamine addiction by an invisible electronic vortex and end up with an altered state of mind? Maybe you don't know what to say. How about some of these?

- "Emancipate yourself from mental slavery" (Bob Marley).
- Do you want to give up your freedom and become a mental slave?
- Do you want to become a dopamine addict for the rest of your life?
- Do you want to allow someone else to control your mind and your life?
- Do you want to let electronic parasites live in your brain and control your behavior? Maybe they will eventually drive you to suicide.
- Do you care about the little children?

Consider Using Legal Remedies

I am not a fan of litigation. However, sometimes litigation is necessary. If you have been injured or if someone in your family has been injured by a driver distracted by their smartphone, perhaps litigation is a way to level the playing field. If you are suffering from anxiety, depression, aggression, or a lowered threshold of patience that was exacerbated by smartphone addiction, you might consider clawing back some of the wealth amassed by tech companies and tech billionaires that knew about the addictive power of dopamine.

You have many choices. You can choose what you do next. On the other hand, you can choose to do nothing. I hope you choose what is best for you and should not let someone else decide for you.

Sincerely,

Jack

Annex A—General Counsel of the Department of Defense

Memorandum for the Secretary of Defense,
September 20, 1977

Subject Experimentation Programs Conducted by the Department of Defense That Had CIA Sponsorship or Participation and That Involved the Administration to Human Subjects of Drugs Intended for Mind-control or Behavior-modification Processes.[464]

GENERAL COUNSEL OF THE DEPARTMENT OF DEFENSE
WASHINGTON, D. C. 20301

September 20, 1977

MEMORANDUM FOR THE SECRETARY OF DEFENSE

> SUBJECT: Experimentation Programs Conducted by the
> Department of Defense That Had CIA Sponsor-
> ship or Participation and That Involved the
> Administration to Human Subjects of Drugs
> Intended for Mind-control or Behavior-
> modification Purposes

On August 8, 1977 you requested that the Office of General Counsel coordinate a search of Department of Defense records to determine the extent of Department of Defense

Page 1 of the September 20, 1977,
Department of Defense Memorandum

https://www.esd.whs.mil/Portals/54/Documents/
FOID/Reading%20Room/NCB/02-A-0846_
RELEASE.pdf

B. **Programs identified**

(1) **Synthesis of analogs of certain central nervous system stimulants**

This project began in 1971 and was terminated in January, 1973. It was performed by a contractor located in Massachusetts. The involvement of the Navy was only as a conduit for funds between the contractor and the Central Intelligence Agency. Some of the funding documents identify this project as a part of project OFTEN.

In December, 1970, the contractor contacted the Central Intelligence Agency project officer directly and suggested research work on two types of drugs: analogs of DOPA and dopamine and analogs of picrotoxin. After the work was undertaken, the contractor added a third aspect, the study of

Page 6 of the September 20, 1977,
Department of Defense Memorandum

https://www.esd.whs.mil/Portals/54/Documents/
FOID/Reading%20Room/NCB/02-A-0846_
RELEASE.pdf

This is a work of the U.S. Government and is not subject to copyright protection in the United States. Foreign copyrights may apply.

Agency association will be confidential." (Doc. No. CIA-1, 3.)

There is no indication in the documents available to the Navy that human testing was performed by the researchers. One of the documents reports: "The relative merits of the synthetic compounds will be determined in mice, and information as to the underlying biochemical basis for the observed pharmacological activities will be deduced from the comparative effects of the various compounds." (Doc. No. CIA-8.)

One of the researcher's progress reports indicates an intention to publish the results of the first phase of this work, on analogs of DOPA and dopamine, at a professional meeting in the fall of 1972 but there is no indication that publication was accomplished. (Doc. No. N-2.)

Page 7 of the September 20, 1977,
Department of Defense Memorandum

https://www.esd.whs.mil/Portals/54/Documents/
FOID/Reading%20Room/NCB/02-A-0846_
RELEASE.pdf

This is a work of the U.S. Government and is not subject to copyright protection in the United States. Foreign copyrights may apply.

Annex B—Copyrights, Government Works, and Substantial Quotations

This annex is included to forestall any lawsuits that may be filed against me to suppress this book. With the details and explanations below, any lawyer that files a lawsuit to suppress publication or distribution of this book will risk being penalized for frivolous litigation. Additionally, we may raise First Amendment issues if booksellers refuse to sell this book based on misinterpretations of "fair use" guidelines regarding copyrighted material.

I include this annex because one publisher tried to force me to remove original documents under the pretense that I exceeded "fair use" guidelines regarding copyrighted material. Quoting original sources is critical to supporting my interpretations of events. Without the ability to quote directly from original sources, skeptics would dismiss this book as a collection of conspiracy theories.

This book uses extensive amounts of "government works" and many "substantial quotations." This annex will address both government works and substantial quotations separately in detail as part I and part II.

Part I—Government Works

Copyright Law of the United States (Title 17) Chapter 1, Section 105. "Subject matter of copyright: United States Government works" states,

> Copyright protection under this title is not available for any work of the United States Government, but the United States Government is not precluded from receiving and holding copyrights transferred to it by assignment, bequest, or otherwise.[465]

This point is explained in more detail by a government task force (CENDI Copyright Working Group) publication *Frequently Asked Questions About Copyright Issues Affecting the U.S. Government* [466]

> Copyright protection is not provided for U.S. Government works under U.S. Copyright Law. Therefore, there is no U.S. Copyright to be transferred. U.S Government employees should inform the publisher of their employment status and should not sign any document purporting to transfer a U.S. copyright as a prerequisite to publication.[467]

"Government works" in this book include the following:

1. Department of Defense memorandums
2. Transcripts from Congressional commissions and hearings
3. Declassified government documents
4. A 2003 paper "Memories for Life" prepared for *LifeLog* on the Defense Advanced Research Projects Agency (DARPA) website.
5. An information sheet for a meeting working on a government-funded project
6. Information posted on several official websites of various U.S. Government agencies and commissions including
   i. The National Reconnaissance Office,
   ii. The Central Intelligence Agency,
   iii. Defense Advance Projects Research Agency,
   iv. The CIA Reading Library,
   v. The Federal Trade Commission,
   vi. The Securities Exchange Commission, and
   vii. Patents (text and drawings) from the US Patent Office.

Government copyrights are explained in the following sources:

1. *Issues Affecting the U.S. Government,* CENDI/2008-1, October 8, 2008[468]

    a. Answers to Question 2.2.2 [469] (The "fair use" limitation found at 17 USC § 107,37 is not defined in the statute and does not provide a bright line rule for determining what is or is not a fair use.)

    b. Answers to Question 2.3.2[470] (No effective transfer of copyright can be made in the U.S. for U.S. Government works [see FAQ Section 3.0] because they are not eligible for copyright protection under the U.S. Copyright Law.)

    c. Answers to Question 3.1.8 [471] (The federal government is not required to provide notice that there is no U.S. copyright on its works.)

    d. Answers to Question 3.2.5 [472] (Federal government employees are not allowed to prepare any document purporting to transfer copyrights to publishers [and by extension authors].)

2. 17 U.S.C., Chapter 1: Subject Matter and Scope of Copyright, Copyright Law of the United States.[473]

    a. 17 U.S.C. Section 105[474]

    b. 17 U.S.C. Section 106[475]

    c. 17 U.S.C. Section 107[476] lists four factors to consider fair use:

        1. The purpose and character of the use, including whether such use, is of a commercial nature or is for nonprofit educational purposes.

        2. The nature of the copyrighted work.

        3. The amount and substantiality of the portion used in relation to the copyrighted work as a whole.

        4. The effect of the use upon the potential market for or value of the copyrighted work.

Part II—Substantial Quotations

Many courts—including the Supreme Court— have affirmed that "substantial quotations" are allowable some situations. In many situations in this book, substantial quotations are necessary due to the sheer magnitude of many separate issues that require Criticism and Commentary.[477]

What is fair use? Question 2.2.2 is answered in *Frequently Asked Questions About Copyright.* "The 'fair use' limitation found at 17 USC § 107, is not defined in the statute and does not provide a bright line rule for determining what is or is not a fair use.[478] Furthermore, these four factors are not to be considered of equal value as explained by the Supreme Court in Harper & Row v. Nation Enterprises, 471 U.S. 539 (1985)[479]

"[40] Effect on the Market. Finally, the Act focuses on "the effect of the use upon the potential market for or value of the copyrighted work." This last factor is undoubtedly the single most important element of fair use.

"Government works" have no market value or potential market value. Therefore, I cannot cause any potential harm to any potential market value or commercial value of "Government works" that I quote. Admittedly, by bringing these "Government works" to the public's attention, I may cause potential harm to the potential market value or the commercial value of some public companies and corporations. However, government laws, and regulations and policies do not conflate the "Government works" and private profits to protect commercial interest of companies and corporations that the government lawfully regulates.

Specifically in the case of the September 20, 1977, Memorandum from the General Counsel for the Department of Defense, I obtained this document from https://www.esd.whs.mil/Portals/54/Documents/FOID/Reading%20Room/NCB/02-A-0846_RELEASE.pdf. As explained above, the US Government does not issue copyright permissions because there are no copyrights for government works. In accordance with government policy to address this issue, I have included their recommended statement, "This is a work of the US

Government and is not subject to copyright protection in the United States. Foreign copyrights may apply."

In the case of "Memories for Life," the copyright permissions may initially appear to be more complicated since the two authors of paper might have been contractors. However, on closer examination of the relevant facts and logic, the copyright permissions are addressed clearly by government policies.

The 2003 paper "Memories for Life" was posted without any copyright notifications for several months on a government website (DARPA's website for Lifelog) as part of a government-funded project. It is, therefore, considered "government work" under copyright laws and regulations. Some might argue that the authors, Andrew Fitzgibbon and Ehud Reiter, might be considered contractors under and are therefore eligible for copyright protection for their 2003 paper. However, chapter 4 of *Frequently Asked Questions About Copyright* clarifies this issue. Under paragraph 4.1 (If a Work Was Created Under a Government Contract, Who Holds the Copyright?) it states, "Under the FAR general data rights clause (FAR 52.227-14), except for works in which the contractor asserts claim to copyright, the Government has unlimited rights in all data first produced in the performance of a contract and all data delivered under a contract unless provided otherwise in the contract."

There is no evidence the authors of "Memories for Life "asserted any claim for copyright. Their paper was posted on a government website (Defense Advanced Research Projects Agency) without any copyright notifications for many months. According to FAR cited in paragraph 4.3, "The contractor must place a copyright notice acknowledging the government sponsorship (including contract number) on the work... If no copyright notice is placed on the work, the Government obtains unlimited rights in the work." Therefore, Andrew Fitzgibbon and Ehud Reiter—the authors of "Memories for Life"—forfeited any copyright protection to their 2003 paper.

If anyone minimizes the arguments above, several courts have previously ruled on these issues. It is, therefore, settled law. I cite verbatim, "[E]ven substantial quotations may constitute fair use in commenting on a published work." The United States District Court for the Northern District of California, Michael Savage v. Council on American-Islamic Relations found that using significant portions of original material is sometimes warranted for criticism and commentary as explained, "17 U.S.C. § 107(3). This factor looks to the quantity and significance of the material used to determine whether the use is reasonably necessary to accomplish the purpose of the defendant's work and whether it supersedes or constitutes the heart of the original work (*Campbell*, 510 U.S. at 586-87). In addition, *the Supreme Court has considered the persuasiveness of the critic's justification for the copying based on the first fair use factor, because the Court recognizes that the extent of permissible copying varies with the purpose and character of the use. Id. Even substantial quotations may constitute fair use in commenting on a published work may constitute fair use in commenting on a published work.*"

In some instances in the book, I use "substantial quotations" for "Criticism and Commentary."[480] Courts have ruled that each situation must be evaluated individually based on many factors. "The policy behind copyright law is not simply to protect the rights of those who produce content"[481] but also to "promote the progress of science and useful arts" U.S. Const. Art. I, § 8, cl. 8. This was reaffirmed by the Supreme Court in HARPER & ROW v. NATION ENTERPRISES, 471 U.S. 539 (1985).

This Supreme Court case affirmed several things as factors (emphasis added):

1. The Court correctly notes that **the effect on the market "is undoubtedly the single most important element of fair use."**

2. **[E]ven substantial quotations might qualify as a fair use** in a review of a published work or a news account of a speech that had been delivered to the public.

3. 17 U.S.C. 107(3) (emphasis added). As the statutory directive implies, **it matters little whether the second author's use is 1- or 100-percent appropriated expression if the taking of that expression had no adverse effect on the copyrighted work.** *See Sony Corp. of America v. Universal City Studios, Inc.,* 464 U.S. 417 (1984) (100-percent of expression taken).

Furthermore, In *Hustler Magazine Inc. v. Moral Majority Inc.*, 796 F.2d 1148, 1151 (9th Cir. 1986), the court affirmed that in "*Harper & Row Publishers*, 471 U.S. at 563. ('The law generally recognizes a greater need to disseminate factual works than works of fiction or fantasy.')" My book seeks to disseminate factual works. Therefore, this factor weighs heavily in favor of disseminating factual works found in the government documents. This is important since it is impossible to obtain copyright permissions from the federal government for government work for two reasons.

Lastly, US Patent 8,095,492—*method and/or system for providing and/or analyzing influence strategies* also needs to be addressed. This patent contains a copyright notice:

> Illustrative embodiments of the present invention are described below. In various embodiments, the present invention may be implemented in part using program source code, using graphical interfaces, or using written tables, manuals, or other instructions. Thus, portions of material included in this submission is copyrightable and copyright is claimed by the inventor. Permission is granted to make copies of the figures, appendix, and any other copyrightable work solely in connection with the making of facsimile copies of this patent document in accordance with applicable law; all other rights are reserved, and all other reproduction, distribution, creation of derivative works based on the contents, public display, and public performance of the application or any part thereof are prohibited by the copyright laws.

This book does not quote or reveal any "source code using graphical interfaces or using written tables, manuals, or other instructions." However, this book does use "substantial quotations." As indicated above, several courts including the Supreme Court have affirmed that substantial quotations are allowable if there is a substantial amount of material that is being quoted for Criticism and Commentary[482]

Endnotes

Note that in several of the government documents listed below, the page numbers printed on the pages may not agree with the page numbers listed in the total PDF. For example, page 71 may be printed on the bottom of the scanned page but the PDF page counter lists the page as 78 of 177.

1   Question 3.1.8, *Frequently Asked Questions About Copyright Issues Affecting the U.S. Government*, CENDI Copyright Working Group, https://www.cendi.gov/publications/04-8copyright.html#325, accessed August 15, 2019.

2   Memorandum for Secretary of Defense, Subject Experimentation Programs Conducted by the Department of Defense That Had CIA Sponsorship or Participation and That Involved to Administration to Human Subjects Intended for Mind control or Behavior-modification Purposes, September 20, 1977, https://www.esd.whs.mil/Portals/54/Documents/FOID/Reading%20Room/NCB/02-A-0846_RELEASE.pdf, accessed September 5, 2019.

3   Hugh Wilford, *The Mighty Wurlitzer: How the CIA Played America*, Harvard University Press, 2008.

4   Plato, *The Allegory Of The Cave*, Republic, VII, 514 a, 2 to 517 a, 7, Translation by Thomas Sheehan, https://web.stanford.edu/class/ihum40/cave.pdf, accessed August 8, 2019.

5   Yoree Koh and Betsy Morris, "Kids Love These YouTube Channels. Who Creates Them Is a Mystery," *Wall Street Journal*, https://www.wsj.com/articles/kids-love-these-youtube-channels-who-creates-them-is-a-mystery-11554975000?mod=searchresults&page=1&pos=1, accessed April 12, 2019.

6   Memorandum for Secretary of Defense, Subject Experimentation Programs Conducted by the Department of Defense That Had CIA Sponsorship or Participation and That Involved to Administration to Human Subjects Intended for Mind-control or Behavior-modification Purposes, September 20, 1977, pp 7-8, https://www.esd.whs.mil/Por-

tals/54/Documents/FOID/Reading%20Room/NCB/02-A-0846_RE-LEASE.pdf, accessed April 6, 2019.

7   Project MKULTRA, The CIA'S Program of Research in Behavioral Modification, Joint Hearing Before the Select Committee on Intelligence and the Subcommittee on Health and Scientific Research of the Committee on Human Resources United States Senate Ninety-Fifth Congress, First Session, August 3, 1977, p 4, https://www.intelligence.senate.gov/sites/default/files/hearings/95mkultra.pdf, accessed July 29, 2019.

8   John Marks, *The Search for the Manchurian Candidate: The CIA and Mind Control*, 1979, W.W. Norton and Company, p 61.

9   Project MKULTRA, The CIA'S Program of Research in Behavioral Modification, p 4, https://www.intelligence.senate.gov/sites/default/files/hearings/95mkultra.pdf.

10   Project MKULTRA, The CIA'S Program of Research in Behavioral Modification, Joint Hearing Before the Select Committee on Intelligence and the Subcommittee on Health and Scientific Research of the Committee on Human Resources United States Senate Ninety-Fifth Congress, First Session, August 3, 1977, https://www.intelligence.senate.gov/sites/default/files/hearings/95mkultra.pdf.

11   Memorandum for Secretary of Defense, Subject Experimentation Programs Conducted by the Department of Defense That Had CIA Sponsorship or Participation and That Involved to Administration to Human Subjects Intended for Mind-control or Behavior-modification Purposes, September 20, 1977, https://www.esd.whs.mil/Portals/54/Documents/FOID/Reading%20Room/NCB/02-A-0846_RELEASE.pdf, accessed September 5, 2019.

12   In-Q-Tel website, https://www.iqt.org/how-we-work/, accessed March 8, 2019.

13   CBS, *Social Media Is a Tool of the CIA. Seriously*, July 11, 2011, https://www.cbsnews.com/news/social-media-is-a-tool-of-the-cia-seriously/, accessed March 31, 2019.

14   Project MKULTRA, The CIA'S Program of Research in Behavioral Modification, p 4, https://www.intelligence.senate.gov/sites/default/files/hearings/95mkultra.pdf.

15   Frederick B. Cohen, US Patent 8,095,492, *Method and/or system for providing and/or analyzing influence strategies,* accessed June 13, 2019.

16   Project MKULTRA, The CIA'S Program of Research in Behavioral Modification, p 4, https://www.intelligence.senate.gov/sites/default/files/hearings/95mkultra.pdf.

17   Frederick B. Cohen, US Patent 8,095,492, *Method and/or system for*

providing and/or analyzing influence strategies, accessed June 13, 2019.

18   David Talbot, Chapter 12, *The Devil's Chessboard: Allen Dulles, The CIA, and the Rise of American's Secret Government*, Harper Perennial, 2015, pp 287–315.

19   Vanessa Grigoriadis, "I Collect People, I Own People, I Can Damage People: The Curious Sociopathy of Jeffrey Epstein," *Vanity Fair*, August 26, 2019, https://www.vanityfair.com/news/2019/08/curious-sociopathy-of-jeffrey-epstein-ex-girlfriends , accessed September 10, 2019.

20   James B. Stewart, August 12, 2019, "The Day Jeffrey Epstein Told Me He Had Dirt on Powerful People," *New York Times*, August 12, 2019, https://www.nytimes.com/2019/08/12/business/jeffrey-epstein-interview.html , accessed September 9, 2019.

21   Anderson Cooper, "What is "brain hacking"? Tech insiders on why you should care," *CBS, 60 Minutes,* June 11, 2017, https://www.cbsnews.com/news/brain-hacking-tech-insiders-60-minutes/, accessed September 15, 2019.

22   Robert H. Lustig, *The Hacking of the American Mind: The Science Behind the Corporate Takeover of Our Bodies and Brains*, Avery (September 12, 2017) 352 pages.

23   Talbot, *The Devil's Chessboard*, p 292–4.

24   In this book, the word smartphone will include not only smartphones but also wearable smart fitness devices, smart video monitors, smart glasses, Google's Alexia, Amazon's Echo Dot, smart cards, the internet, cloud storage, smart cities, and other computers connected to your smartphone.

25   Nicholas Carr, "How Smartphones Hijack Our Minds: Research suggests that as the brain grows dependent on phone technology, the intellect weakens," *The Wall Street Journal*, October 6, 2017, https://www.wsj.com/articles/how-smartphones-hijack-our-minds-1507307811, accessed August 3, 2019.

26   Daniel M. Wegner, Adrian F. Ward, "The Internet Has Become the External Hard Drive for Our Memories," *Scientific American*, December 1, 2013, https://www.scientificamerican.com/article/the-internet-has-become-the-external-hard-drive-for-our-memories/, accessed August 3, 2019.

27   Nicole Martinelli, "Nomophobia Is the Fear Of Losing Your iPhone, But Is It Real?" (Interview), *Cult of Mac*, https://www.cultofmac.com/148086/nomophobia-is-the-fear-of-losing-your-iphone-but-is-it-real-interview/, accessed April 6, 2019.

28   Eileen Brown, "Phone sex: Using our smartphones from the shower

to the sack," ZDNet, July 11, 2013, https://www.zdnet.com/article/phone-sex-using-our-smartphones-from-the-shower-to-the-sack/, accessed April 6, 2019.

29   *Smartphone Addiction Definition, Smartphone Addiction Facts & Phone Usage Statistics, The Definitive Guide (2019 Update),* bankmycell.com, https://www.bankmycell.com/blog/smartphone-addiction, accessed October 7, 2019.

30   Hyung Suk Seo, *Smartphone addiction creates imbalance in brain, study suggests,* Radiological Society of North America, November 30, 2017, https://www.sciencedaily.com/releases/2017/11/171130090041.htm, accessed August 5, 2019.

31   Shakya HB, Christakis NA, *Association of Facebook Use with Compromised Well-Being: A Longitudinal Study,* Am J Epidemiol. 2017 Feb 1;185(3):203-211. doi: 10.1093/aje/kww189, abstract accessed at https://www.ncbi.nlm.nih.gov/pubmed/28093386, accessed September 4, 2019.

32   Mark J Williams and Bryon Adinoff, *The Role of Acetylcholine in Cocaine Addiction,* Neuropsychopharmacology. 2008 Jul; 33(8): 1779–1797, accessed on https://www.ncbi.nlm.nih.gov/pmc/articles/PMC2667818/#R2 , accessed September 15, 2019.

33   Caroline Baum, *Opinion: What's the cost of smartphone addiction?,* https://www.marketwatch.com/story/whats-the-cost-of-smartphone-addiction-2019-03-14, March 14, 2019, accessed March 19, 2019.

34   John P. Thomas, Health Impact News, "Smartphone Addiction Related to Sugar, Narcotics, Alcohol, Pornography, Gambling Addictions" https://healthimpactnews.com/2018/smartphone-addiction-related-to-sugar-narcotics-alcohol-pornography-gambling-addictions, accessed January 29, 2019.

35   Hugh Wilford, *The Mighty Wurlitzer: How the CIA Played America.*

36   Michael Warner, Reviewer, *The Mighty Wurlitzer: How the CIA Played America.* Intelligence in Recent Public Literature, *Hugh Wilford. Cambridge, MA: Harvard University Press, 2008. 342 pages, including notes and index,* https://www.cia.gov/library/center-for-the-study-of-intelligence/csi-publications/csi-studies/studies/vol52no2/intelligence-in-recent-public-literature-1.html, accessed September 15, 2019.

37   The CIA Reading Library, Defense Intelligence Agency, Controlled Offensive Behavior-USSR, U.S. Army, Office of the Surgeon General, John D. LaMothe, Captain, Section IV—Current Research Efforts in Parapharmacology–USSR, page 78 of 177 or page 71 as printed on the page, https://www.cia.gov/library/readingroom/docs/CIA-RDP96-00788R001300010001-7.pdf, accessed August 3, 2019.

38   The CIA Reading Library, Scientific Abstract Goldmakher, P.E.—
Goldshteyn, YE.L., p 47 of 100, https://www.cia.gov/library/read-
ingroom/docs/CIA-RDP86-00513R002200920019-6.pdf, accessed
August 3, 2019.

39   Anderson Cooper, "What is "brain hacking"? Tech insiders on why
you should care," *CBS 60 Minutes*, June 11, 2017, https://www.
cbsnews.com/news/brain-hacking-tech-insiders-60-minutes/, accessed
September 15, 2019.

40   Anderson Cooper, "Hooked on your phone?" *CBS 60 Minutes*, June
11, 2017, https://www.cbsnews.com/news/hooked-on-phones/, accessed September 15, 2019.

41   The Reliable Source, "Quoted: Anderson Cooper on his CIA internship," *The Washington Post*, October 20, 2013, https://www.washing-
tonpost.com/news/reliable-source/wp/2013/10/20/quoted-ander-
son-cooper-on-his-cia-internship/, accessed September 15, 2019.

42   Memorandum for Secretary of Defense, Subject Experimentation
Programs Conducted by the Department of Defense That Had CIA
Sponsorship or Participation and That Involved to Administration to
Human Subjects Intended for DVM; Purposes, September 20, 1977,
https://www.esd.whs.mil/Portals/54/Documents/FOID/Reading%20
Room/NCB/02-A-0846_RELEASE.pdf, accessed September 5, 2019.

43   Project MKULTRA, The CIA'S Program of Research in Behavioral
Modification, p 4, https://www.intelligence.senate.gov/sites/default/
files/hearings/95mkultra.pdf.

44   Anderson Cooper, "What is brain hacking? Tech insiders on why you
should care," *CBS News*, June 11, 2017, https://www.cbsnews.com/
news/what-is-brain-hacking-tech-insiders-on-why-you-should-care/
accessed April 6, 2019.

45   Stephen Foster, *The MKULTRA Compendium, The CIA's Program of
Research in Behavioral Modification*, Lulu, 2009, pp 615.

46   Robert Epstein, June 16, 2019, *Why Google Poses a Serious Threat to
Democracy, and How to End That Threat*, https://www.judiciary.senate.
gov/imo/media/doc/Epstein%20Testimony.pdf, accessed September
15, 2019.

47   Frederick B. Cohen, US Patent 8,095,492, *Method and/or system for
providing and/or analyzing influence strategies,* accessed June 13, 2019.

48   *The Matrix*, Warner Bros. and Village Roadshow Pictures, https://
www.imdb.com/title/tt0133093/, accessed September 16, 2019.

49   Mike Brooks, "Why Do We Feel So Compelled to Check Our
Phones?" *Psychology Today*, https://www.psychologytoday.com/us/blog/
tech-happy-life/201810/why-do-we-feel-so-compelled-check-our-

phones, October 10, 2018, accessed March 4, 2019.

50   Nancy A. Cheever, Larry D. Rosenb, L. Mark Carrierb, Amber Chaveza, *Out of sight is not out of mind: The impact of restricting wire-lessmobile device use on anxiety levels among low, moderate and highusers,* Computers in Human Behavior, Volume 37, August 2014, Pp 290-297, http://www5.csudh.edu/psych/Out_of_sight_is_not_out_of_mind-Cheever,Rosen,Carrier,Chavez_2014.pdf, access July 3, 2019.

51   AndrewLepp, Jacob E.Barkley, Aryn C.Karpinski, "*The relationship between cell phone use, academic performance, anxiety, and Satisfaction with Life in college students,*"Computers in Human Behavior, Volume 31, February 2014, pp 343-350, https://www.sciencedirect.com/science/article/pii/S0747563213003993, accessed July 3, 2019.

52   Russell B. Clayton, Glenn Leshner, Anthony Almond, *The Extended iSelf: The Impact of iPhone Separation on Cognition, Emotion, and Physiology*, January 8, 2015, https://onlinelibrary.wiley.com/doi/full/10.1111/jcc4.12109, accessed July 3, 2019.

53   Anderson Cooper, "What is brain hacking? Tech insiders on why you should care," *CBS News*, June 11, 2017, https://www.cbsnews.com/news/what-is-brain-hacking-tech-insiders-on-why-you-should-care/, accessed April 6, 2019.

54   David Brooks, "How Evil Is Tech?" *New York Times*, November 20, 2017, https://www.nytimes.com/2017/11/20/opinion/how-evil-is-tech.html, accessed April 6, 2019.

55   John Anderer, "*Hurry Up! Modern Patience Thresholds Lower Than Ever Before, Technology To Blame,*" *Study Finds*, 2019, https://www.studyfinds.org/hurry-up-modern-patience-thresholds-lower-than-ever-before-survey-finds, accessed September 3, 2019.

56   Bloomberg, Dopamine Labs, https://www.bloomberg.com/research/stocks/private/snapshot.asp?privcapId=379653117 accessed April 12, 2019.

57   Anderson Cooper, "Brain Hacking," *60 Minutes, CBS News*, Jan 10, 2018, https://www.youtube.com/watch?v=awAMTQZmvPE, accessed April 6, 2019.

58   Anderson Cooper, "Brain Hacking," *60 Minutes, CBS News*, Jan 10, 2018, 13:05, https://www.youtube.com/watch?v=awAMTQZmvPE, accessed April 6, 2019.

59   Roger McNamee, *I invested early in Google and Facebook. Now they terrify me*, USA Today, https://www.usatoday.com/story/opinion/2017/08/08/my-google-and-facebook-investments-made-fortune-but-now-they-menace/543755001/ accessed May 24, 2019.

60   Frederick B. Cohen, US Patent 8,095,492, *Method and/or system for*

providing and/or analyzing influence strategies, accessed June 13, 2019.

61   Roger McNamee, "How Facebook and Google threaten public health—and democracy," *The Guardian*, November 11, 2017, https://www.theguardian.com/commentisfree/2017/nov/11/facebook-google-public-health-democracy, accessed May 24 2019.

62   Olivia Solon, "Ex-Facebook president Sean Parker: site made to exploit human 'vulnerability'," *The Guardian*, November 9, 2017 https://www.theguardian.com/technology/2017/nov/09/facebook-sean-parker-vulnerability-brain-psychology, accessed July 22, 2019.

63   Paul Lewis, Interview with Justin Rosenstein, "Our minds can be hijacked': the tech insiders who fear a smartphone dystopia," *The Guardian*, October 6, 2017, https://www.theguardian.com/technology/2017/oct/05/smartphone-addiction-silicon-valley-dystopia, accessed July 22, 2019.

64   Olivia Solon, "Ex-Facebook president Sean Parker: site made to exploit human 'vulnerability'," *The Guardian*, November 9, 2017 https://www.theguardian.com/technology/2017/nov/09/facebook-sean-parker-vulnerability-brain-psychology, accessed July 22, 2019.

65   Julia Carrie Wong, "Former Facebook executive: social media is ripping society apart," *The Guardian*, https://www.theguardian.com/technology/2017/dec/11/facebook-former-executive-ripping-society-apart, December 12, 2017.

66   Paul Lewis, Interview with Justin Rosenstein, "Our minds can be hijacked': the tech insiders who fear a smartphone dystopia," *The Guardian*, October 6, 2017, https://www.theguardian.com/technology/2017/oct/05/smartphone-addiction-silicon-valley-dystopia, access accessed July 22, 2019.

67   Paul Lewis, "Our minds can be hijacked': the tech insiders who fear a smartphone dystopia," *The Guardian*, October 6, 2017, https://www.theguardian.com/technology/2017/oct/05/smartphone-addiction-silicon-valley-dystopia, accessed July 22, 2019.

68   Frederick B. Cohen, US Patent 8,095,492, *Method and/or system for providing and/or analyzing influence strategies,* accessed June 13, 2019.

69   Royal Society for Public Health, *#StatusOfMindSocial media and young people's mental health and well-being*, May 2017, p 3, https://www.rsph.org.uk/uploads/assets/uploaded/d125b27c-0b62-41c5-a2c0155a8887cd01.pdf , accessed September 12, 2019.

70   National Institute of Drug Abuse (NIDA), https://www.drugabuse.gov/publications/teaching-packets/understanding-drug-abuse-addiction/section-i/6-neurotransmission, accessed April 21, 2019.

71   Dongju Seo, Christopher J. Patrick, and Patrick J. Kennealy, *Role*

of Serotonin and Dopamine System Interactions in the Neurobiology of Impulsive Aggression and its Comorbidity with other Clinical Disorders, Aggress Violent Behav. 2008 Oct; 13(5): 383–395, https://www.ncbi. nlm.nih.gov/pmc/articles/PMC2612120, accessed August 28, 2019.

72   Rajendra D. Badgaiyan, Alan J. Fischman, and Nathaniel M. Alpert, *Dopamine Release During Human Emotional Processing,* Neuroimage. 2009 Oct 1; 47(4): 2041–2045, accessed at https://www.ncbi.nlm. nih.gov/pmc/articles/PMC2740985/, accessed October 6, 2019.

73   Rajendra D. Badgaiyan, *Dopamine is released in the striatum during human emotional processing,* Neuroreport. 2010 Dec 29; 21(18): 1172–1176 , accessed at https://www.ncbi.nlm.nih.gov/pmc/articles/ PMC2997433/, accessed on October 6, 2019.

74   Eric J. Nestler, *The Neurobiology of Cocaine Addiction,* Sci Pract Perspect. 2005 Dec; 3(1): 4–10, Abstract, https://www.ncbi.nlm.nih.gov/ pmc/articles/PMC2851032/, accessed August 2, 2019.

75   Erin S. Calipari and Mark J. Ferris, *Amphetamine Mechanisms and Actions at the Dopamine Terminal Revisited,* J Neurosci. 2013 May 22; 33(21): 8923–8925, https://www.jneurosci.org/content/33/21/8923, accessed August 2, 2019.

76   José De-Sola Gutiérrez, Fernando Rodríguez de Fonseca, and Gabriel Rubio, *Cell-Phone Addiction: A Review,* Front Psychiatry. 2016; 7: 175, accessed at https://www.ncbi.nlm.nih.gov/pmc/articles/ PMC5076301/, accessed on October 6, 2019.

77   Melis MR, Argiolas A., *Dopamine and sexual behavior.* Neurosci Biobehav Rev. 1995 Spring;19(1):19-38, Abstract, https://www.ncbi. nlm.nih.gov/pubmed/7770195/, accessed August 2, 2019.

78   Todd Love, Christian Laier, Matthias Brand, Linda Hatch, and Raju Hajela, *Neuroscience of Internet Pornography Addiction: A Review and Update,* Behav Sci (Basel). 2015 Sep; 5(3): 388–433, accessed at https://www.ncbi.nlm.nih.gov/pmc/articles/PMC4600144/, accessed October 6, 2019.

79   S Kühn, A Romanowski, C Schilling, R Lorenz, C Mörsen, N Seiferth, [T Banaschewski], A Barbot, G J Barker, C Büchel, P J Conrod, J W Dalley, H Flor, H Garavan, B Ittermann, K Mann, J-L Martinot, T Paus, M Rietschel, M N Smolka, A Ströhle, B Walaszek, G Schumann, A Heinz, J Gallinat, and The IMAGEN Consortium, *The neural basis of video gaming,* Transl Psychiatry. 2011 Nov; 1(11): e53, accessed at https://www.ncbi.nlm.nih.gov/pmc/articles/PMC3309473/, accessed on October 6, 2019.

80   Patrick Anselme and Mike J. F. Robinson, *What motivates gambling behavior? Insight into dopamine's role,* Front Behav Neurosci. 2013;

7: 182, accessed at https://www.ncbi.nlm.nih.gov/pmc/articles/ PMC3845016/, accessed October 6, 2019.

81   Joe Cohen, *What Does Dopamine Do? 26 Surprising Dopamine Effects*, July 31, 2019, https://selfhacked.com/blog/dopamine/, accessed August 2, 2019.

82   D. Sutoo, K. Akiyama, *Regulation of brain function by exercise*, Neurobiol Dis. 2003 Jun;13(1):1-14, abstract, https://www.ncbi.nlm.nih. gov/pubmed/12758062, accessed July 3, 2019.

83   DOPAMINE HYDROCHLORIDE- dopamine hydrochloride injection, solution, concentrate, National Institutes of Health, https:// dailymed.nlm.nih.gov/dailymed/drugInfo.cfm?setid=1f306ad2-3606-4525-5a8a-ce78f426c1a2,

84   Erick Trickey, *Inside the Story of America's 19th-Century Opiate Addiction*, smithsonian.com, January 4, 2018, https://www.smithsonian-mag.com/history/inside-story-americas-19th-century-opiate-addiction-180967673/, accessed August 29, 2019.

85   Iltifat Husain, MD, *Key takeaways from the American Academy of Pediatrics tablet and smartphone guidelines for children*, American Academy of Pediatrics (AAP), November 11, 2016, https://www.imedicalapps. com/2016/11/american-academy-pediatrics-tablet-smartphone-guide-lines-children, accessed September 3, 2019.

86   Kent C. Berridge and Morten L. Kringelbach, *Pleasure systems in the brain*, Neuron. 2015 May 6; 86(3): 646–664, doi:10.1016/j.neuron.2015.02.018, accessed at https://www.ncbi.nlm.nih.gov/pmc/ articles/PMC4425246/, accessed October 7, 2019.

87   Adam K. Anderson, *Feeling emotional: the amygdala links emotional perception and experience*, Soc Cogn Affect Neurosci. 2007 Jun; 2(2): 71–72, doi:10.1093/scan/nsm022, https://www.ncbi.nlm.nih.gov/ pmc/articles/PMC2555454/ accessed June 30, 2019.

88   Charles A Marsden, *Dopamine: the rewarding years*, doi: 10.1038/ sj.bjp.0706473, https://www.ncbi.nlm.nih.gov/pmc/articles/ PMC1760752/#bib20, accessed April 8, 2019.

89   Nicole M. Avena, Pedro Rada, and Bartley G. Hoebel· *Evidence for sugar addiction: Behavioral and neurochemical effects of intermittent, excessive sugar intake*, Neurosci Biobehav Rev. 2008; 32(1): 20–39. Abstract, https://www.ncbi.nlm.nih.gov/pmc/articles/PMC2235907/, accessed June 8, 2019.

90   Robert H. Lusting, *The Hacking of the American Mind*, Penguin Random House, 2018, p 29.

91   Robert H. Lusting, *The Hacking of the American Mind*, Penguin Random House, 2018, p 49.

92   N.D. Volkow, J.S. Fowler, G.J. Wang, R. Baler, and F. Telang, *Imaging dopamine's role in drug abuse and addiction*, Neuropharmacology. 2009; 56(Suppl 1): 3–8, Published online 2008 Jun 3. doi:10.1016/j. neuropharm.2008.05.022 https://www.ncbi.nlm.nih.gov/pmc/articles/PMC2696819/, accessed July 28, 2019.

93   L Bevilacqua and D Goldman, *Genes and Addictions*, Clin Pharmacol Ther. 2009 Apr; 85(4): 359–361.

doi: 10.1038/clpt.2009.6, https://www.ncbi.nlm.nih.gov/pmc/articles/PMC2715956/, accessed April 27, 2019.

94   Andrzej Z. Pietrzykowski, and Steven N. Treistman, *The Molecular Basis of Tolerance*, National Institute on Alcohol and Alcoholism, US Department of Health and Human Services, National Institutes of Health, https://pubs.niaaa.nih.gov/publications/arh314/298-309.htm, accessed June 18, 2019.

95   *25 Surprising Facts About Phone Addiction*, Addiction Tips, https://www.addictiontips.net/phone-addiction/phone-addiction-facts/, accessed November 4, 2019.

96   World Health Organization, *Gaming disorder*, September 2018, https://www.who.int/features/qa/gaming-disorder/en/, accessed May 30, 2019.

97   NIDA Blog Team, https://teens.drugabuse.gov/blog/post/tolerance-dependence-addiction-whats-difference, January 12, 2017, accessed June 8, 2019.

98   *Biological Mechanisms of Addiction*, http://www.alcohol-drug.com/biology.php, accessed June 8, 2019.

99   Jason Yanofski, *The Dopamine Dilemma—Part II Could Stimulants Cause Tolerance, Dependence, and Paradoxical Decompensation?*, Innov Clin Neurosci. 2011 Jan; 8(1): 47–53, accessed on https://www.ncbi.nlm.nih.gov/pmc/articles/PMC3036556/, accessed August 27, 2019.

100   National Institute on Drug Abuse, *Opioid Overdose Crisis*, Revised January 2019, https://www.drugabuse.gov/drugs-abuse/opioids/opioid-overdose-crisis, accessed November 18, 2019.

101   CDC/NCHS, National Vital Statistics System, Mortality. CDC WONDER, Atlanta, GA: US Department of Health and Human Services, CDC; 2018. https://wonder.cdc.gov. accessed October 16, 2019.

National Institute on Drug Abuse, *Opioid Overdose Crisis*, Revised January 2019, https://www.drugabuse.gov/drugs-abuse/opioids/opioid-overdose-crisis#one, accessed October 16, 2019.

Mary Jeanne Kreek, *Opioids, dopamine, stress, and the addictions*, Dialogues Clin Neurosci. 2007 Dec; 9(4): 363–378, accessed at https://

www.ncbi.nlm.nih.gov/pmc/articles/PMC3202505/, accessed October 16, 2019.

Methods of making and using dopamine receptor selective antagonists/partial agonists, https://www.ott.nih.gov/technology/e-053-2016-0, accessed October 16, 2019.

Opioid Addiction vs. Opioid Dependence: Key Differences in Symptoms and Treatment You Need to Know, https://www.opiates.com/opioid-addiction-vs-dependence-symptoms-treatment/, accessed June 14, 2019.

102 Scrat Ice Age 1, https://www.youtube.com/watch?v=vCTNioSW730, accessed August 10, 2019.

103 *Smartphone Addiction Signs and Symptoms – Are You a Nomophobe?,* Addiction Resource, June 24th, 2019, https://addictionresource.com/addiction/technology-addiction/smartphone-addiction/smartphone-addiction-signs/, accessed August 14, 2019.

104 National Survey on Drug Use and Health, *2018 NSDUH Detailed Tables,* Substance Abuse and Mental Health Data Archive, https://www.samhsa.gov/data/report/2018-nsduh-detailed-tables, accessed October 7, 2019.

105 *Smartphone Addiction Definition, Smartphone Addiction Facts & Phone Usage Statistics, The Definitive Guide (2019 Update),* bankmycell.com, https://www.bankmycell.com/blog/smartphone-addiction/#chapter1, accessed October 7, 2019.

106 Robert H. Lusting, *The Hacking of the American Mind,* Penguin Random House, 2018, p 25.

107 Dariush DFARHUD, Maryam MALMIR, and Mohammad KHANAHMADI, *Happiness & Health: The Biological Factors- Systematic Review Article,* Iran J Public Health. 2014 Nov; 43(11): 1468–1477, accessed on https://www.ncbi.nlm.nih.gov/pmc/articles/PMC4449495, August 28, 2019.

108 Dongju Seo, Christopher J. Patrick, and Patrick J. Kennealy, *Role of Serotonin and Dopamine System Interactions in the Neurobiology of Impulsive Aggression and its Comorbidity with other Clinical Disorders,* Aggress Violent Behav. 2008 Oct; 13(5): 383–395, accessed on https://www.ncbi.nlm.nih.gov/pmc/articles/PMC2612120, accessed August 28, 2019.

109 Dongju Seo, Christopher J. Patrick, and Patrick J. Kennealy, *Role of Serotonin and Dopamine System Interactions in the Neurobiology of Impulsive Aggression and its Comorbidity with other Clinical Disorders,* Aggress Violent Behav. 2008 Oct; 13(5): 383–395, accessed on https://www.ncbi.nlm.nih.gov/pmc/articles/PMC2612120, accessed August 28, 2019.

110   John Anderer, *Hurry Up! Modern Patience Thresholds Lower Than Ever Before, Technology To Blame,* Study Finds, 2019, https://www.study-finds.org/hurry-up-modern-patience-thresholds-lower-than-ever-before-survey-finds, accessed September 3, 2019.

111   John Anderer, *Serotonin + Confidence Are Key Ingredients For Patience, Study Shows,* 2019, https://www.studyfinds.org/serotonin-confidence-key-ingredients-patience/ accessed September 3, 2019.

112   National Institute of Mental Health, *Prevalence of Major Depressive Episode Among Adults,* https://www.nimh.nih.gov/health/statistics/major-depression.shtml, accessed August 28, 2019.

113   Statisa, *Share of Adults in the United States Who Owned a Smartphone from 2015 to 2018, by Age Group,* https://www.statista.com/statistics/489255/percentage-of-us-smartphone-owners-by-age-group, accessed August 28, 2019.

114   Hackernoon, *How Much Time Do People Spend on Their Mobile Phones in 2017?* May 9, 2017, https://hackernoon.com/how-much-time-do-people-spend-on-their-mobile-phones-in-2017-e5f90a-0b10a6, accessed August 28, 2019.

115   Tim Weiner, *Legacy of Ashes, The History of the CIA*, Anchor Books, New York, 2008, pp 1-54.
Annie Jacobsen, *Operation Paperclip*, Back Bay Books, 2014, p 69.

116   US Army, https://www.army.mil/koreanwar/ accessed January 22, 2019.

117   David Wise and Thomas B Ross, *The Invisible Government*, Random House, 1964, p 102.

118   Weiner, *Legacy of Ashes,* pp 55-90.

119   Harry S. Trumen, *Memoirs*, Vol. II, p. 331. Doubleday and Company, Inc., New York, 1956.

120   Tom Gjelten, *CIA Files Show U.S. Blindsided by Korean War*, NPR, https://www.npr.org/templates/story/story.php?storyId=128092817, June 25, 2010, accessed March 19, 2019.

121   Weiner, *Legacy of Ashes,* pp 9-54.

122   Weiner, *Legacy of Ashes,* pp 1-54.

123   "In Korea, we had atomic weapons, but lost the war and were unable to use those weapons because of a political and psychological climate created by the Communists. The Kremlin today is fighting total war, and this means total not with weapons of physical destruction alone but mental destruction too. The new weapons are for conquest intact of peoples and cities. The future Pearl Harbor sputnik will be used if the situation demands it. But not unless the Kremlin has first succeeded in conquering the characters and minds of a large enough element

of the American people so that it will be fitting itself into the desires and needs of the Communist apparatus, no matter whether they think of themselves as Red or anti-Communist." Edward Hunter, Committee On Un-American Activities, House Of Representatives, Eighty-Fifth Congress, Second Session, March 13, 1958, Printed for the use of the Committee on Un-American Activities, United States Government Printing Office, Washington 1958, http://www.crossroad.to/ Quotes/globalism/Congress.htm, accessed January 22, 2019.

124 John Marks, *The Search for the Manchurian Candidate: The CIA and Mind Control*, 1979, W.W. Norton and Company, p 23.

125 Annie Jacobson, *Operation Paperclip*, Little, Brown and Company, 2014, p 302.

126 Mick Farren, *The CIA Files*, CLB – Quadrillion Publishing Limited, 1999.

127 https://dcas.dmdc.osd.mil/dcas/pages/report_korea_sum.xhtml, accessed January 22, 2019.

128 CRS Report for Congress, June 29, 2010, https://fas.org/sgp/crs/ natsec/RS22926.pdf, accessed January 22, 2019.

129 General Douglas MacAuthur's actions may have hindered the CIA. "[T]he CIA was crippled by MacAuthur, who hated the agency and did his best to ban its officers from the Far East." Tim Weiner, *Legacy of Ashes, The History of the CIA*, Anchor Books, 2008, p 57.

130 Tim Weiner, The New York Times, *Remembering Brainwashing*, https://www.nytimes.com/2008/07/06/weekinreview/06weiner.html, JULY 6, 2008, accessed January 22, 2019.

131 Mick Farren, *The CIA Files: Secrets of "The Company"* Barns and Nobles, p 84, 2004.

132 Edward Hunter, Committee On Un-American Activities, House Of Representatives, Eighty-Fifth Congress, Second Session, March 13, 1958, Printed for the use of the Committee on Un-American Activities, United States Government Printing Office, Washington 1958, http://www.crossroad.to/Quotes/globalism/Congress.htm, accessed January 22, 2019.

133 Plato, *The Allegory Of The Cave*, Republic, VII, 514 a, 2 to 517 a, 7, Translation by Thomas Sheehan, https://web.stanford.edu/class/ ihum40/cave.pdf, accessed August 8, 2019.

134 Edward Hunter, Committee On Un-American Activities, House Of Representatives, Eighty-Fifth Congress, Second Session, March 13, 1958, Printed for the use of the Committee on Un-American Activities, United States Government Printing Office, Washington 1958, http://www.crossroad.to/Quotes/globalism/Congress.htm, accessed

January 22, 2019.

135   Ivan Pavlov Biographical, The Nobel Prize in Physiology or Medicine 1904, https://www.nobelprize.org/prizes/medicine/1904/pavlov/biographical/, accessed November 18, 2019.

136   Mick Farren, *The CIA Files Secrets of 'The Company,'* Quadrillion Publishing Limited, Godalming, England, 1999, p 156.

137   Edward Hunter, *Brainwashing in Red China*, Vanguard Press, 1951, p 10.

138   Mick Farren, *The CIA Files Secrets of 'The Company,'* Quadrillion Publishing Limited, Godalming, England, 1999, p 85.

139   Weiner, *Legacy of Ashes,* pp 55-90.

140   Weiner, *Legacy of Ashes,* pp 87-91.

141   William Joseph Donovan, Major General United States Army, The Arlington National Cemetery Website, http://www.arlingtoncemetery.net/wjodonov.htm, accessed September 13, 2019.

142   Anthony Summers, *Official and Confidential: The Secret Life of J. Edgar Hoover*, ISBN-13: 978-0399138003, (Putnam Adult, 1993) pp 144-155.

143   Weiner, *Legacy of Ashes,* p 8.

144   Anthony Summers, *Official and Confidential: The Secret Life of J. Edgar Hoover*, ISBN-13: 978-0399138003, (Putnam Adult, 1993) pp 241-245.

145   Weiner, *Legacy of Ashes,* pp 25-27.

146   Weiner, *Legacy of Ashes,* p 54.

147   Weiner, *Legacy of Ashes,* p 60.

148   The CIA Reading Library, Taylor Branch, page 66 of 79, article appeared on page 58 of The Washington Monthly, April 1982, https://www.cia.gov/library/readingroom/docs/CIA-RDP90-01137R000100140001-3.pdf, accessed August 3, 2019.

149   Jeffrey T. Richelson, *The Secret History of the U-2*, Foreign Policy, August 15, 2013, https://foreignpolicy.com/2013/08/15/the-secret-history-of-the-u-2/, accessed November 17, 2019.

150   Brian Shul, https://gizmodo.com/the-thrill-of-flying-the-sr-71-blackbird-5511236, accessed April 21, 2019.

151   Ben Rich and Leo Janos, *Skunk Works*, Little, Brown, and Company, 1994, p 207.

152   Lockheed was funded 96.6 million dollars to build five A-12 spy planes that were the predecessors to the SR-12s. Ben Rich and Leo Janos, *Skunk Works*, Little, Brown, and Company, 1994, p 200.

153   National Reconnaissance Office, *Advanced Reconnaissance System*, February 10, 1959, Approved for Release: 2019/03/01

C05119337, https://www.nro.gov/Portals/65/documents/foia/declass/ForAll/051719/F-2019-00053_C05119337.pdf, accessed August 3, 2019.

154   David Wise and Thomas B Ross, *The Invisible Government*, Random House, 1964, P 184–9.

155   CIA Library Reading, *Official History Of The Bay Of Pigs Operation Draft Volume V Cia's Internal Investigation Of The Bay Of Pigs By Jack B. Pfeiffer*, https://www.cia.gov/library/readingroom/docs/C01254908.pdf, accessed August 3, 2019.

156   CIA Library Reading, Room, *Statement of Mr. Allen Dulles, Director of the Central Intelligence Agency to the Senate Foreign Relations Committee*, May 31, 1960, https://www.cia.gov/library/readingroom/docs/DOC_0000009190.pdf, accessed July 23, 2019.

157   CIA Library Reading, Room, *The Taylor Committee Investigation of the Bay of Pigs*, November 9, 1984, https://www.cia.gov/library/readingroom/docs/bop-vol4.pdf, accessed July 23, 2019.

158   Hugh Sidey, *The Lesson John Kennedy Learned From the Bay of Pigs*, Time, April 16, 2001 http://content.time.com/time/nation/article/0,8599,106537,00.html, accessed July 24, 2019.

159   National Reconnaissance Office, Released Records, FOIA for All – Releases, Fiscal Year 2019 - Quarter 2, https://www.nro.gov/Freedom-of-Information-Act-FOIA/Declassified-Records/Other-Public-Releases/FOIA-For-All-Releases/, accessed August 1, 2019.

160   National Reconnaissance Office, *X-20 Dyna Soar*, August 17, 2011, Approved for Release: 2019/02/19 C05118816 https://www.nro.gov/Portals/65/documents/foia/declass/ForAll/051719/F-2019-00053_C05118816.pdf, accessed August 1, 2019.

161   *Soviets hail space hero - Yuri Gagarin the first human in space newsreel archival footage*, publicdomainfootage.com, https://www.youtube.com/watch?v=n0UkT3WKuzU, accessed September 19, 2019.

162   Danielle Muoio, *Google and Alphabet's 20 most ambitious moonshot projects*, Business Insider, February 13, 2016, https://www.businessinsider.com/20-moonshot-projects-by-google-turned-alphabet-2016-2, accessed July 23, 2019.

163   National Intelligence Community, *Report to the National Commission for the Review of the Research and Development Programs of the United Sates Intelligence Community, Unclassified Version*, 2013, https://www.intelligence.senate.gov/sites/default/files/commission_report.pdf, accessed October 1, 2019.

164   CIA website *CIA Technology: Bettering Our Lives*, https://www.cia.

gov/library/video-center/video-transcripts/cia-technology-better-ing-our-lives.html, accessed March 31, 2019.

165 *How we work*, In-Q-Tel website, https://www.iqt.org/how-we-work/, accessed March 8, 2019.

166 *History*, In-Q-Tel website, https://www.iqt.org/our-history/, accessed September 20, 2019.

167 CIA website *The CIA and You: CIA's Contributions to Modern Technology* https://www.cia.gov/news-information/featured-story-archive/2014-featured-story-archive/the-cia-and-you-cia2019s-contributions-to-modern-technology.html, accessed March 31, 2019.

168 Google News, *Google Acquires Keyhole Corp*, October 27, 2004, https://googlepress.blogspot.com/2004/10/google-acquires-key-hole-corp.html , accessed September 21, 2019.

169 Classification of TALENT and KEYHOLE Information, CIA Reading Library https://www.cia.gov/library/readingroom/docs/CIA-RD-P67R00587A000100140024-5.pdf, accessed September 21, 2019.

170

171 *Chapter 8: Aerial photograph interpretation,* https://www.sfu.ca/~hickin/Maps/Chapter%208.pdf, accessed September 22, 2019.

172 http://db.cs.pitt.edu/idm/reports/2000/9631952.html, accessed April 5, 2019.

173 http://db.cs.pitt.edu/idm/reports/2000/9631952.html, accessed April 5, 2019.

174 Tim Weiner, *Blank Check, The Pentagons Black Budget*, Warner Books, 1991, page 68.

175 Samuel Gibbs, *Google buys two more UK artificial intelligence start-ups,* Oct 23, 2014, https://www.theguardian.com/technology/2014/oct/23/google-uk-artificial-intelligence-startups-machine-learning-dark-blue-labs-vision-factory, accessed September 21, 2019.

176 Samuel Gibbs, *Google buys UK artificial intelligence startup Deepmind for £400m,* January 27, 2014, https://www.theguardian.com/technology/2014/jan/27/google-acquires-uk-artificial-intelligence-startup-deep-mind, accessed September 21, 2019.

177 Weiner, *Legacy of Ashes,* 2008, p 32.

178 David Talbot, *The Devil's Chessboard: Allen Dulles, The CIA, and the Rise of America's Secret Government,* Harper Perennial, 2015, p 306.

179 Ben Rich and Leo Janos, *Skunk Works*, Little, Brown, and Company, 1994, p 203.

180 CIA Museum, https://www.cia.gov/about-cia/cia-museum/experi-ence-the-collection/text-version/collection-by-subject/air-america.

html, accessed June 7, 2019.

181   L. Fletcher Prouty, *The Secret Team*, Skyhorse Publishing, 2011, pp347–357.

182   T.D. Allman, How the CIA Helped Disney Conquer Florida, The Daily Beast Company, https://www.thedailybeast.com/how-the-cia-helped-disney-conquer-florida, accessed March 31, 2019.

183   Orlikow v. United States, 682 F. Supp. 77 (D.D.C. 1988), https://law.justia.com/cases/federal/district-courts/FSupp/682/77/1583126/, accessed April 27, 2019.

184   Memorandum for Secretary of Defense, Subject Experimentation Programs Conducted by the Department of Defense That Had CIA Sponsorship or Participation and That Involved to Administration to Human Subjects Intended for Mind-control or Behavior-modification Purposes, September 20, 1977, https://www.esd.whs.mil/Portals/54/Documents/FOID/Reading%20Room/NCB/02-A-0846_RELEASE.pdf, accessed September 5, 2019.

185   Nicholas Carlson, "At Last—The Full Story of How Facebook Was Founded," *Business Insider,* March 5, 2010, http://www.businessinsider.com/how-facebook-was-founded-2010-3?op=1, accessed September 7, 2019.

186   Ben Mezrich, *The Accidental Billionaires: The Founding of Facebook A Tale of Sex, Money, Genius, and Betrayal* (New York: Doubleday, 2009).

187   Dave Gershgorn, *The Unbreakable Genius of Mark Zuckerberg*, Popular Science, August 23, 2016, https://www.popsci.com/mark-zuckerberg, accessed September 2, 2019.

188   Jayson DeMers, *Wanna Become an Entrepreneurial Rock Star? Here's How,* Entrepreneur, https://www.entrepreneur.com/article/281822, accessed September 7, 2019.

189   CBS, *Social Media Is a Tool of the CIA. Seriously,* July 11, 2011, https://www.cbsnews.com/news/social-media-is-a-tool-of-the-cia-seriously/, accessed March 31, 2019.

190   Hugh Wilford, *The Mighty Wurlitzer: How the CIA Played America.*

191   Appeal from the United States District Court for the District of Delaware in Case No. 08-CV-0862, Judge Leonard P. Stark, Decided: May 8, 2012, p 5, https://www.courtlistener.com/pdf/2012/05/08/leader_technologies_inc._v._facebook_inc..pdf , accessed September 9, 2019.

192   Appeal from the United States District Court for the District of Delaware in Case no. 08-CV -0862, Judge Leonard P. Stark, page 6, https://leader.com/docs/Leader-v-Facebook-APPEAL-Opening-Brief-25-Jul-2011.pdf , accessed September 9, 2019.

193   Michael T. McKibben and Jeffrey R. Lamb, US Patent 7,139,761, *Dynamic association of electronically stored information with iterative workflow changes,* November 21, 2006, accessed September 9, 2019.

194   Appeal from the United States District Court for the District of Delaware in Case no. 08-CV -0862, Judge Leonard P. Stark, pp 3–4, https://leader.com/docs/Leader-v-Facebook-APPEAL-Opening-Brief-25-Jul-2011.pdf , accessed September 9, 2019.

195   Appeal from the United States District Court for the District of Delaware in Case no. 08-CV -0862, Judge Leonard P. Stark, page 2, https://leader.com/docs/Leader-v-Facebook-APPEAL-Opening-Brief-25-Jul-2011.pdf , accessed September 9, 2019.

196   Appeal from the United States District Court for the District of Delaware in Case no. 08-CV -0862, Judge Leonard P. Stark, page 3, https://leader.com/docs/Leader-v-Facebook-APPEAL-Opening-Brief-25-Jul-2011.pdf , accessed September 9, 2019.

197   Microsoft Research, *MyLifeBits Project,* November 5, 2002, The Wayback Machine, https://web.archive.org/web/20021105002300/http://research.microsoft.com/barc/mediapresence/mylifebits.aspx , accessed September 9, 2019.

198   Anne Eisenberg, "WHAT'S NEXT; Memories as Heirlooms Logged Into a Database," New *York Times,* March 20, 2003, https://www.nytimes.com/2003/03/20/technology/what-s-next-memories-as-heirlooms-logged-into-a-database.html, accessed September 9, 2019.

199   Gordon Bell, Jim Gemmell, Roger Lueder, *Personal TP System for Everything Inspired by Memex www.MyLifeBits.com* , MicroSoft Research, https://web.archive.org/web/20060426192154/http://research.microsoft.com/~gbell/Bell_MyLifeBits_Talk_SIGMOD_050614_web.ppt , accessed September 9, 2019.

200   Katharine A. Kaplan, "Facemash Creator Survives Ad Board," *The Harvard Crimson,* November 19, 2003, http://www.thecrimson.com/article/2003/11/19/facemash-creator-survives-ad-board-the/, accessed January 8, 2015.

201   Nicholas Carlson, "In 2004, Mark Zuckerberg Broke into a Facebook User's Private Email Account," *Business Insider,* March 5, 2010, http://www.businessinsider.com/how-mark-zuckerberg-hacked-into-the-harvard-crimson-2010-3, accessed September 7, 2019. If that link is taken down, try https://web.archive.org/web/20180410142515/http://www.businessinsider.com/how-mark-zuckerberg-hacked-into-the-harvard-crimson-2010-3/, accessed November 18, 2019. If they take down both link, we can tell they are very sensitive about the facts getting out.

202   Ibid.

203   Dominic Rushe, "Facebook IPO sees Winklevoss twins heading for $300m fortune," *The Guardian,* February 2, 2012, http://www.theguardian.com/technology/2012/feb/02/facebook-ipo-winklevoss-300m-fortune, accessed September 7, 2019.

204   Dominic Rushe, "Facebook IPO sees Winklevoss twins heading for $300m fortune," *The Guardian,* February 2, 2012, http://www.theguardian.com/technology/2012/feb/02/facebook-ipo-winklevoss-300m-fortune, accessed September 7, 2019.

205   Leanna B. Ehrlich, "Are the Winklevoss Twins Assholes? Summers Might Think So," July 20, 2011, Flyby The blog of *The Harvard Crimson*, https://www.thecrimson.com/flyby/article/2011/7/20/larry-summers-winklevoss-asshole/ , accessed September 7, 2019.

206   Zoe Greenberg, "How Jeffrey Epstein made himself into a 'Harvard man,'" *The Boston Globe*, July 11, 2019, https://www.bostonglobe.com/metro/2019/07/11/how-jeffrey-epstein-made-himself-into-harvard-man/m672RjwFJFwWOVzF9WRNjO/story.html, accessed September 7, 2019.

207   Jaquelyn M. Scharnick, "Mogul Donor Gives Harvard More Than Money Reclusive investor Epstein forges intellectual and financial connections with University," *The Harvard Crimson*, May 1, 2003, https://www.thecrimson.com/article/2003/5/1/mogul-donor-gives-harvard-more-than/?page=single , accessed September 7, 2019.

208   Jaquelyn M. Scharnick, "Mogul Donor Gives Harvard More Than Money Reclusive investor Epstein forges intellectual and financial connections with University," *The Harvard Crimson*, May 1, 2003, https://www.thecrimson.com/article/2003/5/1/mogul-donor-gives-harvard-more-than/?page=single , accessed September 7, 2019.

209   Rob Price, "Mark Zuckerberg once met Jeffrey Epstein at a dinner hosted by LinkedIn cofounder Reid Hoffman that Elon Musk also attended," *Business Insider*, Jul. 17, 2019, https://www.businessinsider.com/elon-musk-mark-zuckerberg-jeffrey-epstein-reid-hoffman-report-2019-7, accessed September 8, 2019.

210   Sarah McBride, *Epstein Arrest Leaves Top Technology Figures Racing to Distance Themselves.* Bloomberg, July 31, 2019, https://www.bloomberg.com/news/articles/2019-07-31/jeffrey-epstein-arrest-spurs-tech-figures-to-distance-themselves, accessed September 8, 2019.

211   James B. Stewart, Matthew Goldstein and Jessica Silver-Greenberg, "Jeffrey Epstein Hoped to Seed Human Race With His DNA," *The New York Times*, July 31, 2019, https://www.nytimes.com/2019/07/31/business/jeffrey-epstein-eugenics.html accessed Sep-

tember 16, 2019.

212   Vanessa Grigoriadis, "I Collect People, I Own People, I Can Damage People": The Curious Sociopathy of Jeffrey Epstein, *Vanity Fair*, August 26, 2019, https://www.vanityfair.com/news/2019/08/curious-sociopathy-of-jeffrey-epstein-ex-girlfriends, accessed September 10, 2019.

213   James B. Stewart, August 12, 2019, "The Day Jeffrey Epstein Told Me He Had Dirt on Powerful People," *New York Times*, August 12, 2019, https://www.nytimes.com/2019/08/12/business/jeffrey-epstein-interview.html , accessed September 9, 2019.

214   Ali Watkins, "Jeffrey Epstein Is Indicted on Sex Charges as Discovery of Nude Photos Is Disclosed," *The New York Times*, https://www.nytimes.com/2019/07/08/nyregion/jeffrey-epstein-charges.html?module=inline, accessed September 7, 2019.

215   Patricia Mazzei, "Years After Plea Deal in Sex Case, Jeffrey Epstein's Accusers Will Get Their Day in Court," *The New York Times*, November 29, 2018, https://www.nytimes.com/2018/11/29/us/jeffrey-epstein-acosta-florida-sex-abuse.html , accessed September 7, 2019.

216   Annie Karni, Eileen Sullivan and Noam Scheiber, "Acosta to Resign as Labor Secretary Over Jeffrey Epstein Plea Deal," *The New York Times*, July 12, 2019, https://www.nytimes.com/2019/07/12/us/politics/acosta-resigns-trump.html , accessed September 7, 2019.

217   Vicky Ward, *Jeffrey Epstein's Sick Story Played Out for Years in Plain Sight*, The Daily Beast, Updated Aug. 19, 2019, https://www.thedailybeast.com/jeffrey-epsteins-sick-story-played-out-for-years-in-plain-sight?ref=scroll, accessed November 18, 2019.

218   Anthony Summers, *Official and Confidential: The Secret Life of J. Edgar Hoover*, ISBN-13: 978-0399138003, (Putnam Adult, 1993) pp 241-245.

219   Reuters, *Court releases documents related to financier Jeffrey Epstein*, August 9, 2019, https://www.reuters.com/article/people-jeffrey-epstein-documents-idUSL2N25511X , accessed November 17, 2019.

220   Amy Robach, "VIDEO: Leaked ABC News Insider Recording EXPOSES #EpsteinCoverup "We had Clinton, We had Everything" Project Veritas, Youtube, November 5, 2019,https://www.youtube.com/watch?v=3lfwkTsJGYA, accessed November 5, 2019.

221   Megyn Kelly, Twitter, 4:04 PM, November 17, 2019, https://twitter.com/megynkelly/status/1196217668044505088 , accessed November 18, 2019.

222   Disney, ABC News, https://disney.fandom.com/wiki/ABC_News , accessed November 18, 2019

223   T.D. Allman, How the CIA Helped Disney Conquer Florida, The Daily Beast Company, https://www.thedailybeast.com/how-the-cia-helped-disney-conquer-florida, accessed March 31, 2019.

224   Julia Fioretti, "Facebook 'tramples European privacy law': Belgian watchdog," *Reuters,* http://www.reuters.com/article/2015/05/15/us-facebook-eu-privacy-idUSKBN0O00XW20150515, accessed May 18, 2015.

225   Julian Hattem, "Facebook claims 'a bug' made it track nonusers," *The Hill,* April 9, 2015, http://thehill.com/policy/technology/238399-facebook-claims-a-bug-made-it-track-people-not-on-facebook, accessed April 10, 2015.

226   Federal Trade Commission, *Facebook Settles FTC Charges That It Deceived Consumers By Failing To Keep Privacy Promises,* November 29, 2011, https://www.ftc.gov/news-events/press-releases/2011/11/facebook-settles-ftc-charges-it-deceived-consumers-failing-keep, accessed June 25, 2019.

227   Homeland Security Newswire, *Using Social Media to Analyze, Thwart Terrorist Activity,* News Wire Publications, 26 July 2019, http://www.homelandsecuritynewswire.com/dr20190726-using-social-media-to-analyze-thwart-terrorist-activity, accessed August 17, 2019.

228   CBS, *Social Media Is a Tool of the CIA. Seriously,* July 11, 2011, https://www.cbsnews.com/news/social-media-is-a-tool-of-the-cia-seriously/, accessed March 31, 2019.

229   Wayback Machine, archive record of DARPA LIFELOG, https://web.archive.org/web/20040203001603/https:/www.darpa.mil/ipto/Programs/lifelog/index.htm, accessed April 3, 2019.

230   Wayback Machine, archive record of DARPA LIFELOG, https://web.archive.org/web/20040203001603/https:/www.darpa.mil/ipto/Programs/lifelog/index.htm, accessed April 3, 2019.

231   Andrew Fitzgibbon and Ehud Reiter, *"Memories for life" Managing information over a human lifetime,* 2003, http://www.nesc.ac.uk/esi/events/Grand_Challenges/proposals/Memories.pdf (The original URL has been taken down. You can still access it by putting the URL into the web.archive.org) or use this URL https://web.archive.org/web/20040331065003/http://www.nesc.ac.uk/esi/events/Grand_Challenges/proposals/Memories.pdf, accessed May 10, 2019.

232   Andrew Fitzgibbon and Ehud Reiter, *"Memories for life" Managing information over a human lifetime,* 2003, http://www.nesc.ac.uk/esi/events/Grand_Challenges/proposals/Memories.pdf (The original URL has been taken down. You can still access it by putting the URL into the web.archive.org) or use this URL https://web.archive.org/

web/20040331065003/http://www.nesc.ac.uk/esi/events/Grand_ Challenges/proposals/Memories.pdf, accessed May 10, 2019.

233   Reuters, as reported by New York Times, Pentagon Explores a New Frontier In the World of Virtual Intelligence, https://www. nytimes.com/2003/05/30/us/pentagon-explores-a-new-fron- tier-in-the-world-of-virtual-intelligence.html?src=pm&gwh=C- 39232292790FE3ED00B94B118A98CA1&gwt=pay, accessed March 31, 2019.

234   Jon Russell , *Microsoft is closing the social network you forgot it ever launched,* Tech Crunch, March 3, 2017, https://techcrunch. com/2017/03/07/microsoft-socl-close/, accessed August 5, 2019.

235   Wired Staff, *Pentagon Kills Lifelog Project,* https://www.wired. com/2004/02/pentagon-kills-lifelog-project/, Wired, February 4, 2004, accessed April 3, 2019.

236   Facebook, https://www.facebook.com/185150934832623/ posts/402581153089599/?_fb_noscript=1, accessed April 3, 2019.

237   Robert Gellman and Pam Dixon, *Data Brokers and the Federal Gov- ernment: A New Front in the Battle for Privacy Opens | Introduction and Background,* World Privacy Forum, October 30, 2013, https:// www.worldprivacyforum.org/2013/10/report-data-brokers-and-gov- ernment-introduction-and-background/, PDF, *Data Brokers and the Federal Government: A New Front in the Battle for Privacy Opens, http:// www.worldprivacyforum.org/wp-content/uploads/2013/10/WPF_Data- BrokersPart3_fs.pdf,* accessed September 17, 2019.

238   Dave Gershgorn, The Unbreakable Genius of Mark Zuckerberg, Pop- ular Science, August 23, 2016, https://www.popsci.com/mark-zucker- berg, accessed September 2, 2019.

239   Andrew Fitzgibbon and Ehud Reiter, *"Memories for life" Managing information over a human lifetime,* 2003, http://www.nesc.ac.uk/esi/ events/Grand_Challenges/proposals/Memories.pdf (The original URL has been taken down. You can still access it by putting the URL into the web.archive.org) or use this URL https://web.archive.org/ web/20040331065003/http://www.nesc.ac.uk/esi/events/Grand_ Challenges/proposals/Memories.pdf, accessed May 10, 2019

240   Roger Parloff, *Peter Thiel disagrees with you,* Fortune, September 4, 2014, http://fortune.com/2014/09/04/peter-thiels-contrarian-strate- gy/, accessed May 10, 2019.

241   Peter Thiel Biography, The Famous People, https://www.thefamous- people.com/profiles/peter-thiel-42197.php, accessed August 31, 2019.

242   Roger Parloff, *Peter Thiel disagrees with you,* Fortune, September 4, 2014, http://fortune.com/2014/09/04/peter-thiels-contrarian-strate-

gy/, accessed May 10, 2019.

243   Edmondson, James Larry, https://www.fjc.gov/history/judges/edmondson-james-larry, accessed September 5, 2019.

244   Peter Thiel Biography, The Famous People, https://www.thefamouspeople.com/profiles/peter-thiel-42197.php, accessed August 31, 2019.

245   Best Law Firms, https://bestlawfirms.usnews.com/profile/sullivan-cromwell-llp/rankings/12959, accessed May 10, 2019.

246   Kim Zetter, *April 13, 1953: CIA OKs MK-ULTRA Mind-Control Tests,* Wired, April 13, 2010 https://www.wired.com/2010/04/0413mk-ultra-authorized/, accessed August 31, 2019.

247   Stephen Kinzer, "The Brothers; John Foster Dulles, Allen Dulles, and Their Secret World War," *Times Books,* 2013, pp 39-41, 59–60, 62, 64, 86–87, 326.

248   Lizette Chapman, *Peter Thiel's Palantir Wins $876 Million U.S. Army Contract,* Bloomberg, March 9, 2018, https://www.bloomberg.com/news/articles/2018-03-09/peter-thiel-s-palantir-wins-876-million-u-s-army-contract, accessed May 10, 2019.

249   Jacques Peretti, "Palantir: the 'special ops' tech giant that wields as much real-world power as Google," *The Guardian,* November 24, 2017, https://www.theguardian.com/world/2017/jul/30/palantir-peter-thiel-cia-data-crime-police, accessed September 13, 2019.

250   Peter Waldman, Lizette Chapman, and Jordan Robertson, *Palantir Knows Everything About You,* Bloomberg, https://www.bloomberg.com/features/2018-palantir-peter-thiel/, April 19, 2018, accessed April 3, 2019.

251   Julianne Pepitone and Stacy Cowley, *Facebook's first big investor, Peter Thiel, cashes out,* CNN, https://money.cnn.com/2012/08/20/technology/facebook-peter-thiel/index.html, accessed April 5, 2019

252   David Kirkpatrick, *The Facebook Effect,* Simon and Schuster, 2010, p 89.

253   Reuters, *Peter Thiel sells most of remaining Facebook stake,* https://www.reuters.com/article/us-facebook-stake-idUSKBN1DM2BQ, Reuters, November 22, 2017 accessed April 3, 2019

254   Nicholas Confessore and Matthew Rosenberg, "Spy Contractor's Idea Helped Cambridge Analytica Harvest Facebook Data," *New York Times,* March 27, 2018, https://www.nytimes.com/2018/03/27/us/cambridge-analytica-palantir.html, accessed May 10, 2019.

255   Project MKULTRA, The CIA'S Program of Research in Behavioral Modification, p 74/394, https://www.intelligence.senate.gov/sites/default/files/hearings/95mkultra.pdf.

256   Alex Verkhivker, *Zuckerberg Testifies Before Congress And Now Ev-*

eryone Is Worried Tech's Too Dominant https://www.forbes.com/
sites/alexverkhivker/2018/04/23/zuckerberg-testifies-before-con-
gress-and-now-everyone-is-worried-techs-too-dominant/ Forbes, April
23, 2018, accessed April 3, 2019.

257   Facebook, *A Privacy-Focused Vision for Social Networking* March 6,
2019, https://newsroom.fb.com/news/2019/03/vision-for-social-net-
working/ accessed June 7, 2019.

258   Michael Liedtke, *Zuckerberg promises a privacy-friendly Facebook,
sort of,* APNews, https://apnews.com/c7c5997c63b543f4bb75fcfcb-
c30fd40, accessed June 7, 2019.

259   United States District Court Northern District of California
San Francisco Division, CASE NO. 3:18-MD-02843-VC, Memorandum Of Law In Support of Motion Of Defendant Facebook, Inc.
to Dismiss Plaintiffs' First Amended Consolidated Complaint, Filed
March 15, 2019, https://www.cand.uscourts.gov/filelibrary/3676/Mo-
tion-to-Dismiss-Amended-Complaint-261-1.pdf, accessed November
18, 2019.

260   Sam Biddle, "In Court, Facebook Blames Users for Destroying Their
Own Right to Privacy," *The Intercept*, June 14, 2019, https://theinter-
cept.com/2019/06/14/facebook-privacy-policy-court/ accessed June
14, 2019.

261   Sam Biddle, "In Court, Facebook Blames Users for Destroying Their
Own Right to Privacy," *The Intercept*, June 14 2019, https://theinter-
cept.com/2019/06/14/facebook-privacy-policy-court/ accessed June
14, 2019.

262   https://assets.documentcloud.org/docu-
ments/6153329/05-29-2019-Facebook-Inc-Consumer-Privacy.txt

263   Wired Staff, *Pentagon Kills Lifelog Project*, https://www.wired.
com/2004/02/pentagon-kills-lifelog-project/, Wired, February 4,
2004, accessed April 3, 2019.

264   Facebook, https://www.facebook.com/185150934832623/
posts/402581153089599/?_fb_noscript=1, accessed April 3, 2019.

265   Facebook SEC Form S-1, Registration Statement, February 1, 2012,
p 2,
https://www.sec.gov/Archives/edgar/
data/1326801/000119312512034517/d287954ds1.ht-
m#toc287954_2, accessed August 12, 2019.

266   Nicholas Carlson, *"Embarrassing And Damaging" Zuckerberg IMs
Confirmed By Zuckerberg, The New Yorker,* https://www.businessinsider.
com/embarrassing-and-damaging-zuckerberg-ims-confirmed-by-zuck-
erberg-the-new-yorker-2010-9, accessed May 10, 2019.

267   "Mark Zuckerberg," *BrainyQuote,* accessed April 10, 2015, http://www.brainyquote.com/search_results.html?q=zuckerberg&pg=3.

268   Francesca Fontana, *Lawsuits Against Facebook Over Data Privacy Issues Are Piling Up,* The Street, March 29, 2018 https://www.thestreet.com/story/14536213/1/everyone-who-is-suing-facebook-for-cambridge-analytica.html, accessed June 7, 2019.

269   Micah Singleton, *11,000 people sue Facebook over privacy violations,* The Daily Dot, Last updated December 11, 2015, https://www.dailydot.com/debug/facebook-class-action-lawsuit/, accessed September 13, 2019,

270   Adam Conway, *Fined €250,000 A Day Until it Complies with EU Privacy Laws,* xdadevelopers, February 17, 2018, accessed June 7, 2019.

271   Natasha Lomas, Facebook fined €1.2M for privacy violations in Spain , https://techcrunch.com/2017/09/11/facebook-fined-e1-2m-for-privacy-violations-in-spain/, accessed June 7, 2019.

272   Reuters, EU fines Facebook €110m over misleading WhatsApp data 18 May 2017, https://www.rte.ie/news/business/2017/0518/876113-facebook-fined-by-commission/, accessed June 7, 2019.

273   Federal Trade Commission, *FTC Imposes $5 Billion Penalty and Sweeping New Privacy Restrictions on Facebook,* FTC's new 20-year settlement order, https://www.ftc.gov/news-events/press-releases/2019/07/ftc-imposes-5-billion-penalty-sweeping-new-privacy-restrictions, accessed July 28, 2019.

274   Federal Trade Commission, FTC's new 20-year settlement order, https://www.ftc.gov/system/files/documents/cases/182_3109_facebook_order_filed_7-24-19.pdf, accessed July 28, 2019.

275   David Mikkelson, *Facebook Listens?,* Snopes, https://www.snopes.com/fact-check/facebook-listens/, accessed August 15, 2019.

276   Sarah Frier, *Facebook Paid Contractors to Transcribe Users' Audio Chats,* Bloomberg, August 13, 2019, https://www.bloomberg.com/news/articles/2019-08-13/facebook-paid-hundreds-of-contractors-to-transcribe-users-audio?srnd=premiumhttps://www.bloomberg.com/news/articles/2019-08-13/facebook-paid-hundreds-of-contractors-to-transcribe-users-audio?srnd=premium, accessed August 13, 2019.

277   Aliasgar Mumtaz Husain and Yali X,, US Patent Application 20180167677, June 14, 2018, http://appft.uspto.gov/netacgi/nph-Parser?Sect1=PTO2&Sect2=HITOFF&p=1&u=%2Fnetahtml%2FPTO%2Fsearch-bool.html&r=1&f=G&l=50&co1=AND&d=PG01&s1=20180167677&OS=20180167677&RS=20180167677, accessed August 15, 2019.

278   Sarah Frier, *Facebook Paid Contractors to Transcribe Users' Audio Chats*, Bloomberg, August 13, 2019, https://www.bloomberg.com/news/articles/2019-08-13/facebook-paid-hundreds-of-contractors-to-transcribe-users-audio?srnd=premiumhttps://www.bloomberg.com/news/articles/2019-08-13/facebook-paid-hundreds-of-contractors-to-transcribe-users-audio?srnd=premium, accessed August 13, 2019.

279   Sarah Frier, *Facebook Paid Contractors to Transcribe Users' Audio Chats*, Bloomberg, August 13, 2019, https://www.bloomberg.com/news/articles/2019-08-13/facebook-paid-hundreds-of-contractors-to-transcribe-users-audio?srnd=premiumhttps://www.bloomberg.com/news/articles/2019-08-13/facebook-paid-hundreds-of-contractors-to-transcribe-users-audio?srnd=premium, accessed August 13, 2019.

280   *Facebook is secretly using your iPhone's camera as you scroll your feed*, https://thenextweb.com/apps/2019/11/12/facebook-camera-ios-iphone/, accessed November 18, 2019.

281   *Facebook is secretly using your iPhone's camera as you scroll your feed*, https://thenextweb.com/apps/2019/11/12/facebook-camera-ios-iphone/, accessed November 18, 2019.

282   Kathleen Michon, Tobacco Litigation: History & Recent Developments, https://www.nolo.com/legal-encyclopedia/tobacco-litigation-history-and-development-32202.html

283   Danny Hakim, Roni Caryn Rabin and William K. Rashbaum, *Lawsuits Lay Bare Sackler Family's Role in Opioid Crisis,* The New York Times, April 1, 2019, https://www.nytimes.com/2019/04/01/health/sacklers-oxycontin-lawsuits.html, accessed June 18, 2019.

284   Jan Hoffman, "Purdue Pharma and Sacklers Reach $270 Million Settlement in Opioid Lawsuit," *The New York Times*, March 26, 2019, https://www.nytimes.com/2019/03/26/health/opioids-purdue-pharma-oklahoma.html, accessed June 18, 2019.

285   Sara Randazzo and Jared S. Hopkins, "Johnson & Johnson Ordered to Pay $572 Million in Oklahoma Opioid Case," *Wall Street Journal*, August 26, 2019, https://www.wsj.com/articles/johnson-johnson-ordered-to-pay-572-million-in-oklahoma-opioid-case-11566850079, accessed August 26, 2019.

286   Howard L. Fields and Elyssa B. Margolis, *Understanding Opioid Reward,* Trends Neurosci. 2015 Apr; 38(4): 217–225., accessed on HHS Public access, https://www.ncbi.nlm.nih.gov/pmc/articles/PMC4385443/, accessed August 26, 2019.

287   Sara Randazzo and Jared S. Hopkins, "Johnson & Johnson Ordered to Pay $572 Million in Oklahoma Opioid Case," *Wall Street Journal*, August 26, 2019, https://www.wsj.com/articles/johnson-johnson-or-

dered-to-pay-572-million-in-oklahoma-opioid-case-11566850079, accessed August 26, 2019.

288 The Editorial Board, "An Oklahoma Opioid Stickup: The $572 million ruling greatly expands product liability tort law," *The Wall Street Journal*, https://www.wsj.com/articles/an-oklahoma-opioid-stickup-11566861973?mod=hp_opin_pos_1, accessed August 26, 2019.

289 Kathleen Michon, Tobacco Litigation: History & Recent Developments, https://www.nolo.com/legal-encyclopedia/tobacco-litigation-history-and-development-32202.html, accessed September 5, 2019.

290 Bill Thornton, Alyson Faires, Maija Robbins, Eric Rollins, *The Mere Presence of a Cell Phone May be Distracting: Implications for Attention and Task Performance,* Social Psychology (2014), 45, pp. 479-488. https://doi.org/10.1027/1864-9335/a000216.

291 Department of Transportation Summary of Statistical Findings, 2019, https://crashstats.nhtsa.dot.gov/Api/Public/ViewPublication/812700, accessed July 28, 2019.

292 Justia, *Actual and Proximate Cause*, https://www.justia.com/injury/negligence-theory/actual-and-proximate-cause/, accessed July 28, 2019.

293 National Safety Council, *NSC releases latest injury and fatality statistics and trends,* March 25, 2014, https://www.nsc.org/Portals/0/Documents/NewsDocuments/2014-Press-Release-Archive/3-25-2014-Injury-Facts-release.pdf, accessed September 17, 2019.

294 Consumer Reports, *Android vs. Apple*, October 2019, p 31.

295 Justia, *Actual and Proximate Cause*, https://www.justia.com/injury/negligence-theory/actual-and-proximate-cause/, accessed July 28, 2019.

296 Nancy A. Cheever, Larry D. Rosenb, L. Mark Carrierb, Amber Chaveza, *Out of sight is not out of mind: The impact of restricting wirelessmobile device use on anxiety levels among low, moderate and highusers,* Computers in Human Behavior, Volume 37, August 2014, Pp 290-297, http://www5.csudh.edu/psych/Out_of_sight_is_not_out_of_mind-Cheever,Rosen,Carrier,Chavez_2014.pdf, accessed July 3, 2019.

297 AndrewLepp. Jacob E.Barkley, Aryn C.Karpinski, *The relationship between cell phone use, academic performance, anxiety, and Satisfaction with Life in college students,* Computers in Human Behavior, Volume 31, February 2014, Pp 343-350, https://www.sciencedirect.com/science/article/pii/S0747563213003993, accessed July 3, 2019.

298 Russell B. Clayton, Glenn Leshner, Anthony Almond, *The Extended iSelf: The Impact of iPhone Separation on Cognition, Emotion, and Physi-*

ology, January 8, 2015, , accessed July 3, 2019.

299   Anderson Cooper, "What is "brain hacking"? Tech insiders on why you should care," *CBS News*, June 11, 2017, https://www.cbsnews.com/news/what-is-brain-hacking-tech-insiders-on-why-you-should-care/, accessed April 6, 2019.

300   Kurt Wagner, *In the Garage Where Google Was Born*, Mashable, September 27, 2013, https://mashable.com/2013/09/27/google-garage-anniversary/, accessed August 14, 2019.

301   Daniel Henninger. "The Google Syndrome," *The Wall Street Journal*, September 4, 2019, https://www.wsj.com/articles/the-google-syndrome-11567636819?mod=hp_opin_pos_1, September 5, 2019.

302   CBS, *Social Media Is a Tool of the CIA. Seriously*, July 11, 2011, https://www.cbsnews.com/news/social-media-is-a-tool-of-the-cia-seriously/, accessed March 31, 2019.

303   Noah Shachtman, *Exclusive: Google, CIA Invest in 'Future' of Web Monitoring*, July 28, 2010, https://www.wired.com/2010/07/exclusive-google-cia/ , accessed September 9, 2019.

304   Recorded Future, https://www.recordedfuture.com/about/, accessed September 9, 2019.

305   Cale Guthrie Weissman, *Inside the company that can predict the future by analyzing every piece of information on the web*, Business Insider, May 26, 2015, https://www.businessinsider.com/recorded-future-can-predict-the-future-by-analyzing-everything-on-the-web-2015-5, accessed September 9, 2019.

306   Nafeez Ahmed, *How the CIA made Google, Part One and Two*, Medium Insurge Intelligence, https://medium.com/insurge-intelligence/how-the-cia-made-google-e836451a959e and https://medium.com/insurge-intelligence/why-google-made-the-nsa-2a80584c9c1, accessed August 14, 2019.

307   Brian Friel, *Start Your Idea Engines*, Government Media Executive Group LLC. https://www.govexec.com/magazine/features/2006/05/start-your-idea-engines/21898/, accessed April 5, 2019.

308   Bhavani Thuraisingham, https://www.utdallas.edu/~bxt043000/, accessed June 25, 2019.

309   Nafeez Ahmed, *How the CIA made Google, Part Two*, Medium Insurge Intelligence, https://medium.com/insurge-intelligence/how-the-cia-made-google-e836451a959ehttps://medium.com/insurge-intelligence/why-google-made-the-nsa-2a80584c9c1, accessed October 1, 2019.

310   Seymour M. Hersh, "The Coming Wars What the Pentagon can now do in secret," *The New Yorker*, January 16, 2005, https://www.newyorker.com/magazine/2005/01/24/the-coming-wars, accessed October 1,

2019.

311   MITRE website, https://www.mitre.org/about/corporate-overview, accessed April 12, 2019.

312   Jeff Carlson, "Nellie Ohr Testimony Confirms Her Work for the CIA," *The Epoch Times*, March 13, 2019 Updated: June 14, 2019, https://www.theepochtimes.com/nellie-ohr-testimony-confirms-her-work-for-the-cia_2836812.html, accessed July 17, 2019.

313   **Ms. Ohr:** *Starting in 2000, I did some part-time contracting for Mitre, which is a contract—*
Rep. Jordan: *I'm sorry, I didn't hear you.*
Ms. Ohr: *Mitre. Mitre Corporation, which in turn had contracts with U.S. Government clients.*
Rep. Jordan: *Got it.*
Ms. Ohr: *Through most of 2008. And then starting in 2008, I worked for Open Source Works.*

314   Central Intelligence Agency Directorate of Intelligence, November 16, 2010, https://fas.org/irp/cia/product/iran-space.pdf, accessed July 17, 2019.

315   Bhavani Thuraisingham, *Big Data: Have we seen it before?*, https://www.utdallas.edu/~bxt043000/Motivational-Articles/Big_Data-Have_we_seen_it_before.pdf, accessed June 25, 2019.

316   Bhavani Thuraisingham, *Big Data: Have we seen it before?*, https://www.utdallas.edu/~bxt043000/Motivational-Articles/Big_Data-Have_we_seen_it_before.pdf, accessed June 25, 2019.

317   Nafeez Ahmed, *How the CIA made Google, Part One and Two,* Medium Insurge Intelligence, https://medium.com/insurge-intelligence/how-the-cia-made-google-e836451a959e and https://medium.com/insurge-intelligence/why-google-made-the-nsa-2a80584c9c1, accessed August 14, 2019.

318   https://www.utdallas.edu/~bxt043000/Motivational-Articles/Big_Data-Have_we_seen_it_before.pdf, accessed April 5, 2019.

319   Memorandum for Secretary of Defense, Subject Experimentation Programs Conducted by the Department of Defense That Had CIA Sponsorship or Participation and That Involved to Administration to Human Subjects Intended for Mind-control or Behavior-modification Purposes, September 20, 1977, https://www.esd.whs.mil/Portals/54/Documents/FOID/Reading%20Room/NCB/02-A-0846_RELEASE.pdf, accessed September 5, 2019.

320   David Hart, *On the Origins of Google*, https://www.nsf.gov/discoveries/disc_summ.jsp?cntn_id=100660, accessed April 5, 2019.

321   Sergey Brin, Rajeev Motwani, Lawrence Page, Terry Winograd, *What*

can you do with a Web in your Pocket, National Science Foundation, http://db.cs.pitt.edu/idm/reports/1998/9631952.html, accessed April 5, 2019.

322   Sergey Brin, Rajeev Motwani, Lawrence Page, Terry Winograd, *What can you do with a Web in your Pocket* National https://citeseerx.ist.psu.edu/viewdoc/download?doi=10.1.1.36.2806&rep=rep1&type=pdf, accessed April 5, 2019.

323   Science Foundation, http://db.cs.pitt.edu/idm/reports/1998/9631952.html, accessed April 5, 2019.

324   National Science Foundation, Award Abstract #9411306, The Stanford Integrated Digital Library Project, Last Amendment Date October 5, 1998, https://web.archive.org/web/20190509124147/https://www.nsf.gov/awardsearch/showAward?AWD_ID=9411306, accessed November 18, 2019.

325   http://db.cs.pitt.edu/idm/reports/2000/9631952.html, accessed April 5, 2019.

326   Tony Romm, "The Justice Department is preparing a potential antitrust investigation of Google," *The Washington Post*, May 31, 2019, https://www.washingtonpost.com/technology/2019/06/01/justice-department-is-preparing-potential-antitrust-investigation-google/, accessed September 18, 2019.

327   Jonathan Shieber, *Forty-nine states and the District of Columbia are pushing an antitrust investigation against Google,* Tech Crunch, September 9, 2019, https://techcrunch.com/2019/09/09/forty-nine-states-and-the-district-of-columbia-are-pushing-an-antitrust-investigation-against-google/, accessed September 18, 2019.

328   Jeffrey D. Ullman, NSF Grant IRI-96-31952 Data Warehousing and Decision Support, http://db.cs.pitt.edu/idm/reports/2000/9631952.html, accessed November 18, 2019.

329   HSToday, January 26, 2006, https://www.hstoday.us/kimery-report/while-fending-off-doj-subpoena-google-continues-longstanding-relationship-with-us-intelligence/, accessed April 5, 2019.

330   Weiner, *Legacy of Ashes,* p 64.

331   Karen McVeigh, "CIA sued over 1950s 'murder' of government scientist plied with LSD, The Guardian, November 28, 2012, https://www.theguardian.com/world/2012/nov/29/cia-lawsuit-scientist-1950s-death, accessed October 8, 2019.

332   Joseph B. Treaster, "Ex-C.I.A. Aide Says Scientist Who Died Knew About Experiments with LSD," *The New York Times*, July 18, 1975, https://www.nytimes.com/1975/07/18/archives/excia-aide-says-scien-

tist-who-died-knew-about-experiments-with-lsd.html, accessed August 7, 2019.

333 John Marks, *The Search for the Manchurian Candidate: The CIA and Mind Control*, 1979, W.W. Norton and Company, p 60.

334 Talbot, *The Devil's Chessboard*, pp 287–315.

335 Weiner, *Legacy of Ashes*, pp 72–4.

336 The Rockefeller Commission, June 1975, https://history-matters. com/archive/church/rockcomm/contents.htm, accessed September 20, 2019.

337 Senate Select Committee to Study Governmental Operations with Respect to Intelligence Activities, https://www.cop.senate.gov/artand-history/history/common/investigations/ChurchCommittee.htm, accessed September 30, 2019.

338 John Marks, *The Search for the Manchurian Candidate: The CIA and Mind Control*, 1979, W.W. Norton and Company, p 91.

339 Jeffrey St. Clair - Alexander Cockburn *The CIA's House of Horrors: Frank Olson's Fatal Trip*, November 10, 2017, https://www.counter-punch.org/2017/11/10/the-cias-house-of-horrors-frank-olsons-fatal-trip/, accessed July 31, 2019.

340 John Marks, *The Search for the Manchurian Candidate: The CIA and Mind Control*, 1979, W.W. Norton and Company, p 91.

341 National Geographic - CIA Secret Experiments Documentary, 42: 33 time mark, https://www.youtube.com/watch?v=7Afjf2ZgGZE&feature=youtu.be, accessed May 21, 2019.

342 StevenWarRan Backstage, https://stevenwarran-backstage.blogspot. com/2014/11/august-8-2002-press-conference.html, accessed August 17, 2019.

343 John Marks, *The Search for the Manchurian Candidate: The CIA and Mind Control*, 1979, W.W. Norton and Company, p 92.

344 The New York Times Archives, "Family in LSD Case Gets Ford Apology," *The New York Times*, July 22, 1975, https://www.nytimes. com/1975/07/22/archives/family-in-lsd-case-gets-ford-apology-family-in-lsd-death-case-gets.html, accessed July 29, 2019.

345 James Risen, "Suit Planned Over Death of Man C.I.A. Drugged," *The New York Times*, November 26, 2012, https://www.nytimes. com/2012/11/27/us/family-of-frank-olson-man-drugged-by-cia-plans-suit.html, accessed July 31, 2019.

346 S.Res.21 — 94th Congress (1975-1976), Passed Senate amended (01/27/1975), https://www.congress.gov/bill/94th-congress/senate-res-olution/21, accessed June 15, 2019.

347   Project MKULTRA, The CIA'S Program of Research in Behavioral Modification, https://www.intelligence.senate.gov/sites/default/files/hearings/95mkultra.pdf.

348   Memorandum for Secretary of Defense, Subject Experimentation Programs Conducted by the Department of Defense That Had CIA Sponsorship or Participation and That Involved to Administration to Human Subjects Intended for Mind-control or Behavior-modification Purposes, September 20, 1977, pp 2-3, https://www.esd.whs.mil/Portals/54/Documents/FOID/Reading%20Room/NCB/02-A-0846_RELEASE.pdf, accessed April 6, 2019.

349   Project MKULTRA, The CIA'S Program of Research in Behavioral Modification, p 74/394, https://www.intelligence.senate.gov/sites/default/files/hearings/95mkultra.pdf.

350   Project MKULTRA, The CIA'S Program of Research in Behavioral Modification, page 74/394 or PDF counter 77 of 173, https://www.intelligence.senate.gov/sites/default/files/hearings/95mkultra.pdf.

351   Project MKULTRA, The CIA'S Program of Research in Behavioral Modification, page 74/394 or PDF counter 77 of 173, https://www.intelligence.senate.gov/sites/default/files/hearings/95mkultra.pdf.

352   Talbot, *The Devil's Chessboard*, p 292-4.

353   James Risen, "Suit Planned Over Death of Man C.I.A. Drugged," *The New York Times*, November 26, 2012, https://www.nytimes.com/2012/11/27/us/family-of-frank-olson-man-drugged-by-cia-plans-suit.html, accessed September 20, 2019.

354   Talbot, *The Devil's Chessboard*, p 294.

355   Project MKULTRA, The CIA'S Program of Research in Behavioral Modification, p 75/395, https://www.intelligence.senate.gov/sites/default/files/hearings/95mkultra.pdf.

356   John Marks, *The Search for the Manchurian Candidate: The CIA and Mind Control*, 1979, W.W. Norton and Company, p 77.

357   John Marks, *The Search for the Manchurian Candidate: The CIA and Mind Control*, 1979, W.W. Norton and Company, p 86.

358   Project MKULTRA, The CIA'S Program of Research in Behavioral Modification, p 77/397, https://www.intelligence.senate.gov/sites/default/files/hearings/95mkultra.pdf, https://www.esd.whs.mil/Portals/54/Documents/FOID/Reading%20Room/NCB/02-A-0846_RELEASE.pdf, accessed July 28, 2019.

359   Stephen Kinzer, "From mind control to murder? How a deadly fall revealed the CIA's darkest secrets," *The Guardian*, September 6, 2019, https://www.theguardian.com/us-news/2019/sep/06/from-mind-control-to-murder-how-a-deadly-fall-revealed-the-cias-darkest-secrets,

accessed September 20, 2019.

360 Project MKULTRA, The CIA'S Program of Research in Behavioral Modification, p 78/398, https://www.intelligence.senate.gov/sites/default/files/hearings/95mkultra.pdf.

361 Project MKULTRA, The CIA'S Program of Research in Behavioral Modification, pp 77/397 to 79/399, https://www.intelligence.senate.gov/sites/default/files/hearings/95mkultra.pdf.

362 Project MKULTRA, The CIA'S Program of Research in Behavioral Modification, pp 77/397 to 79/399, https://www.intelligence.senate.gov/sites/default/files/hearings/95mkultra.pdf.

363 Stephen Kinzer, "From mind control to murder? How a deadly fall revealed the CIA's darkest secrets," *The Guardian*, September 6, 2019, https://www.theguardian.com/us-news/2019/sep/06/from-mind-control-to-murder-how-a-deadly-fall-revealed-the-cias-darkest-secrets, accessed September 20, 2019.

364 James Risen, "Suit Planned Over Death of Man C.I.A. Drugged," *The New York Times*, November 26, 2012, https://www.nytimes.com/2012/11/27/us/family-of-frank-olson-man-drugged-by-cia-plans-suit.html, accessed August 7, 2019.

365 John Marks, *The Search for the Manchurian Candidate: The CIA and Mind Control*, 1979, W.W. Norton and Company, p 92-3.

366 Stephen Kinzer, "From mind control to murder? How a deadly fall revealed the CIA's darkest secrets," *The Guardian*, September 6, 2019, https://www.theguardian.com/us-news/2019/sep/06/from-mind-control-to-murder-how-a-deadly-fall-revealed-the-cias-darkest-secrets, accessed September 20, 2019.

367 Frederick B. Cohen, US Patent 8,095,492, *Method and/or system for providing and/or analyzing influence strategies,* accessed June 13, 2019.

368 David Talbot, *The Devil's Chessboard*, p 291.

369 David Talbot, *The Devil's Chessboard*, p 553.

370 Project MKULTRA, The CIA'S Program of Research in Behavioral Modification, https://www.intelligence.senate.gov/sites/default/files/hearings/95mkultra.pdf.

371 Memorandum for Secretary of Defense, Subject Experimentation Programs Conducted by the Department of Defense That Had CIA Sponsorship or Participation and That Involved to Administration to Human Subjects Intended for Mind-control or Behavior-modification Purposes, September 20, 1977, pp 7-8, https://www.esd.whs.mil/Portals/54/Documents/FOID/Reading%20Room/NCB/02-A-0846_RELEASE.pdf, accessed April 6, 2019.

372 Geremia Zito Marinosci, Edoardo De Robertis, Giuseppe De Ben-

edictis, and Ornella Piazza, *Dopamine Use in Intensive Care: Are We Ready to Turn it Down?,* Transl Med UniSa. 2012 Sep-Dec; 4: 90–94, Published online 2012 Oct 11, https://www.ncbi.nlm.nih.gov/pmc/articles/PMC3728808/, accessed August 2, 2019.

373   Memorandum for Secretary of Defense, Subject Experimentation Programs Conducted by the Department of Defense That Had CIA Sponsorship or Participation and That Involved to Administration to Human Subjects Intended for Mind-control or Behavior-modification Purposes, September 20, 1977, pp 7-8, https://www.esd.whs.mil/Portals/54/Documents/FOID/Reading%20Room/NCB/02-A-0846_RELEASE.pdf, accessed April 6, 2019.

374   Project MKULTRA, The CIA'S Program of Research in Behavioral Modification, p 3, https://www.intelligence.senate.gov/sites/default/files/hearings/95mkultra.pdf.

375   Weiner, *Legacy of Ashes,* p 74.

376   Project MKULTRA, The CIA'S Program of Research in Behavioral Modification, p 9, https://www.intelligence.senate.gov/sites/default/files/hearings/95mkultra.pdf.

377   Project MKULTRA, The CIA'S Program of Research in Behavioral Modification, p 69/389, https://www.intelligence.senate.gov/sites/default/files/hearings/95mkultra.pdf.
David Talbot, *The Devil's Chessboard*, pp 292-4.

378   Project MKULTRA, The CIA'S Program of Research in Behavioral Modification, p 3, https://www.intelligence.senate.gov/sites/default/files/hearings/95mkultra.pdf.

379   Frederick B. Cohen, US Patent 8,095,492, *Method and/or system for providing and/or analyzing influence strategies,* accessed June 13, 2019.

380   Frederick B. Cohen, US Patent 8,095,492, *Method and/or system for providing and/or analyzing influence strategies,* accessed June 13, 2019.

381   Project MKULTRA, The CIA'S Program of Research in Behavioral Modification, pp 5-22, https://www.intelligence.senate.gov/sites/default/files/hearings/95mkultra.pdf.

382   Project MKULTRA, The CIA'S Program of Research in Behavioral Modification, p 4, https://www.intelligence.senate.gov/sites/default/files/hearings/95mkultra.pdf, accessed July 29, 2019.

383   Project MKULTRA, The CIA'S Program of Research in Behavioral Modification, https://www.intelligence.senate.gov/sites/default/files/hearings/95mkultra.pdf, p 3, accessed April 3, 2019.

384   Foster, *The MKULTRA Compendium,* pp 17-19 and 601-613.

385   Project MKULTRA, The CIA'S Program of Research in Behavioral Modification, pp 67/387 – 72/392, https://www.intelligence.senate.

gov/sites/default/files/hearings/95mkultra.pdf, accessed August 1, 2019.

386 Foster, *The MKULTRA Compendium,* pp 601-613.

387 Project MKULTRA, The CIA'S Program of Research in Behavioral Modification, p 13, https://www.intelligence.senate.gov/sites/default/files/hearings/95mkultra.pdf, accessed April 3, 2019.

388 Project MKULTRA, The CIA'S Program of Research in Behavioral Modification, p 10-11, https://www.intelligence.senate.gov/sites/default/files/hearings/95mkultra.pdf, accessed April 3, 2019.

389 Bathurst, James, Atomic Consciousness Abridgement, W. Manning, London, 1909.

390 Hendricus G. Loos, US Patent, 6,091,994, http://patft.uspto.gov/netacgi/nph-Parser?Sect1=PTO1&Sect2=HITOFF&d=PALL&p=1&u=%2Fnetahtml%2FPTO%2Fsrchnum.htm&r=1&f=G&l=50&s1=6,091,994.PN.&OS=PN/6,091,994&RS=PN/6,091,994, accessed June 10, 2019.

391 US Patent 6,017,302, http://patft.uspto.gov/netacgi/nph-Parser?-Sect1=PTO1&Sect2=HITOFF&d=PALL&p=1&u=%2Fnetahtml%2FPTO%2Fsrchnum.htm&r=1&f=G&l=50&s1=6,017,302.PN.&OS=PN/6,017,302&RS=PN/6,017,302 , accessed September 30, 2019.

392 Hendricus G. Loos, US Patent, 6,081,744, http://patft.uspto.gov/netacgi/nph-Parser?Sect1=PTO1&Sect2=HITOFF&d=PALL&p=1&u=%2Fnetahtml%2FPTO%2Fsrchnum.htm&r=1&f=G&l=50&s1=6,081,744.PN.&OS=PN/6,081,744&RS=PN/6,081,744, accessed June 10, 2019.

393 Hendricus G. Loos, US Patent, 6,238,333, http://patft.uspto.gov/netacgi/nph-Parser?Sect1=PTO1&Sect2=HITOFF&d=PALL&p=1&u=%2Fnetahtml%2FPTO%2Fsrchnum.htm&r=1&f=G&l=50&s1=6,238,333.PN.&OS=PN/6,238,333&RS=PN/6,238,333, accessed June 10, 2019.

394 Hendricus G. Loos, US Patent, 5,800,481, http://patft.uspto.gov/netacgi/nph-Parser?Sect1=PTO1&Sect2=HITOFF&d=PALL&p=1&u=%2Fnetahtml%2FPTO%2Fsrchnum.htm&r=1&f=G&l=50&s1=5,800,481.PN.&OS=PN/5,800,481&RS=PN/5,800,481, accessed June 10, 2019.

395 Hendricus G. Loos, US Patent, 6,506,148, http://patft.uspto.gov/netacgi/nph-Parser?Sect1=PTO1&Sect2=HITOFF&d=PALL&p=1&u=%2Fnetahtml%2FPTO%2Fsrchnum.htm&r=1&f=G&l=50&s1=6,506,148.PN.&OS=PN/6,506,148&RS=PN/6,506,148, accessed June 10, 2019.

396   Hendricus G. Loos, US Patent, 6,167,304, http://patft.
uspto.gov/netacgi/nph-Parser?Sect1=PTO1&Sect2=HI-
TOFF&d=PALL&p=1&u=%2Fnetahtml%2FPTO%2Fsrchnum.
htm&r=1&f=G&l=50&s1=6,167,304.PN.&OS=PN/6,167,304&RS
=PN/6,167,304, accessed June 10, 2019.

397   Hendricus G. Loos, US Patent, 6,167,304, http://patft.
uspto.gov/netacgi/nph-Parser?Sect1=PTO1&Sect2=HI-
TOFF&d=PALL&p=1&u=%2Fnetahtml%2FPTO%2Fsrchnum.
htm&r=1&f=G&l=50&s1=6,167,304.PN.&OS=PN/6,167,304&RS
=PN/6,167,304 accessed June 10, 2019.

398   Hendricus G. Loos, US Patent, 6,167,304, http://patft.
uspto.gov/netacgi/nph-Parser?Sect1=PTO1&Sect2=HI-
TOFF&d=PALL&p=1&u=%2Fnetahtml%2FPTO%2Fsrchnum.
htm&r=1&f=G&l=50&s1=6,167,304.PN.&OS=PN/6,167,304&RS
=PN/6,167,304 accessed June 10, 2019.

399   The list of all 15 patents from same inventor:
6,506,148 nervous system manipulation by electromagnetic fields
from monitors
6,238,333 remote magnetic manipulation of nervous systems
6,167,304 pulse variability in electric field manipulation of nervous
systems
6,091,994 pulsative manipulation of nervous systems
6,081,744 electric fringe field generator for manipulating nervous
systems
6,017,302 subliminal acoustic manipulation of nervous systems
5,935,054 magnetic excitation of sensory resonances
5,899,922 manipulation of nervous systems by electric fields
5,800,481 thermal excitation of sensory resonances
5,782,874 method and apparatus for manipulating nervous systems
4,475,927 bipolar fog abatement system
4,361,403 multiple wavelength instrument for measurement of particle size distributions
4,338,030 dispersive instrument for measurement of particle size
distributions
4,245,909 optical instrument for measurement of particle size distributions
5,995,954 method and apparatus for associative memory

400   US Patent 6,506,148, http://patft.uspto.gov/netacgi/nph-Parser?-
Sect1=PTO1&Sect2=HITOFF&d=PALL&p=1&u=%2Fnetahtm-
l%2FPTO%2Fsrchnum.htm&r=1&f=G&l=50&s1=6,506,148.PN
.&OS=PN/6,506,148&RS=PN/6,506,148, accessed September 30,

2019.

401   Hendricus G. Loos, US Patent, 6,506,148, http://
patft.uspto.gov/netacgi/nph-Parser?Sect1=PTO1&-
Sect2=HITOFF&d=PALL&p=1&u=%2Fnetahtml%2FPTO%2Fs-
rchnum.htm&r=1&f=G&l=50&s1=6,506,148.PN.&OS=PN/6,506,1
48&RS=PN/6,506,148, accessed June 10, 2019.

402   Ryan Waniata and Kris Wouk, LED vs. LCD TVs explained:
What's the difference?, May 7, 2019, https://www.digitaltrends.com/
home-theater/led-vs-lcd-tvs/, accessed July 1, 2019.

403   Hendricus G. Loos, US Patent, 6,506,148, http://patft.
uspto.gov/netacgi/nph-Parser?Sect1=PTO1&Sect2=HI-
TOFF&d=PALL&p=1&u=%2Fnetahtml%2FPTO%2Fsrchnum.
htm&r=1&f=G&l=50&s1=6,506,148.PN.&OS=PN/6,506,148&RS
=PN/6,506,148, accessed June 10, 2019.

404   Hendricus G. Loos, US Patent, 6,238,333, http://patft.
uspto.gov/netacgi/nph-Parser?Sect1=PTO1&Sect2=HI-
TOFF&d=PALL&p=1&u=%2Fnetahtml%2FPTO%2Fsrchnum.
htm&r=1&f=G&l=50&s1=6,238,333.PN.&OS=PN/6,238,333&RS
=PN/6,238,333, accessed June 10, 2019.

405   Hendricus G. Loos, US Patent, 6,238,333, http://patft.
uspto.gov/netacgi/nph-Parser?Sect1=PTO1&Sect2=HI-
TOFF&d=PALL&p=1&u=%2Fnetahtml%2FPTO%2Fsrchnum.
htm&r=1&f=G&l=50&s1=6,238,333.PN.&OS=PN/6,238,333&RS
=PN/6,238,333, accessed June 10, 2019.

406   Government Interests, Method and apparatus for associative memory,
US Patent 5,995,954 "This invention was made with Government
support provided by the Defense Advanced Research Projects Agency,
ARPA Order 6429, through Contract DAAH01-88-C-0887, issued
by the U.S. Army Missile Command. The Government has certain
rights in the invention."

407   Method and apparatus for associative memory, US Patent 5,995,954
http://patft.uspto.gov/netacgi/nph-Parser?Sect1=PTO1&Sect2=HI-
TOFF&d=PALL&p=1&u=%2Fnetahtml%2FPTO%2Fsrchnum.
htm&r=1&f=G&l=50&s1=5,995,954.PN.&OS=PN/5,995,954&RS
=PN/5,995,954, accessed September 30, 2019.

408   Hendricus G. Loos, US Patents 4,245,909, 4,338,030, 4,361,403,
4,475,927, accessed June 10, 2019.

409   Frederick B. Cohen, US Patent 8,095,492, *Method and/or system for
providing and/or analyzing influence strategies*, accessed June 13, 2019.

410   Anderson Cooper, "What is brain hacking? Tech insiders on why you
should care," *CBS News*, June 11, 2017, https://www.cbsnews.com/

news/what-is-brain-hacking-tech-insiders-on-why-you-should-care/ accessed April 6, 2019.

411   Cornell Law School, Legal Information Institute, https://www.law. cornell.edu/uscode/text/18/part-I/chapter-77, accessed July 22, 2019.

412   New Orleans History Facts and Timeline, http://www.world-guides. com/north-america/usa/louisiana/new-orleans/new_orleans_history. html, accessed April 23, 2019.

413   Mary Bates, "Meet 5 'zombie' parasites that mind-control their hosts," National Geographic, October 22, 2018, https://www.nationalgeo-graphic.com/news/2018/10/141031-zombies-parasites-animals-sci-ence-halloween/, accessed September 30, 2019.

414   Lynne Malcolm, *Neuroplasticity: how the brain can heal itself,* April 21, 2015, https://www.abc.net.au/radionational/programs/allinthemind/ neuroplasticity-and-how-the-brain-can-heal-itself/6406736, accessed September 13, 2019.

415   Anderson Cooper, "What is brain hacking? Tech insiders on why you should care," *CBS News,* June 11, 2017, https://www.cbsnews.com/ news/what-is-brain-hacking-tech-insiders-on-why-you-should-care/ accessed April 6, 2019.

416   Frederick B. Cohen, US Patent 8,095,492, *Method and/or system for providing and/or analyzing influence strategies,* accessed June 13, 2019.

417   Frederick B. Cohen, US Patent 8,095,492, *Method and/or system for providing and/or analyzing influence strategies,* accessed June 13, 2019.

418   Artificial Intelligence (A-W Series in Computer science) 3rd (third) Edition by Winston published by Addison Wesley (1992), https://www.amazon.com/Artificial-Intelligence-Computer-science-Winston-published/dp/B00EKYW2TY/ref=sr_1_3?key-words=%22Artificial+Intelligence%22+Winston%2C+Addison-Wes-ley%2C+1992&qid=1560447089&s=gateway&sr=8-3

419   "Winston, P. "Artificial Intelligence," Addison-Wesley, 1992, cited by examiner." Frederick B. Cohen, US Patent 8,095,492, *Method and/or system for providing and/or analyzing influence strategies,* accessed June 13, 2019.

420   Patent Application US Patent Office, 20070156814, filed July 5, 2007, http://appft.uspto.gov/netacgi/nph-Parser?Sect1=PTO2&-Sect2=HITOFF&p=1&u=%2Fnetahtml%2FPTO%2Fsearch-bool. html&r=1&f=G&l=50&co1=AND&d=PG01&s1=20070156814&O S=20070156814&RS=20070156814

421   Martin Chilton, *How the CIA brought Animal Farm to the screen,* Tele-graph Media Group, January 21, 2016, https://www.telegraph.co.uk/ books/authors/how-cia-brought-animal-farm-to-the-screen/, accessed

October 4, 2019.

422 John Patterson, *The caring, sharing CIA,* October 4, 2001, https://www.theguardian.com/film/2001/oct/05/artsfeatures, accessed April 28, 2019.

423 CIA, Entertainment Industry Liaison, https://www.cia.gov/offices-of-cia/public-affairs/entertainment-industry-liaison/index.html, accessed June 26, 2019.

424 Project MKULTRA, The CIA'S Program of Research in Behavioral Modification, pp 5–22, https://www.intelligence.senate.gov/sites/default/files/hearings/95mkultra.pdf.

425 Project MKULTRA, The CIA'S Program of Research in Behavioral Modification, pp 5–22, 72, 94, 169, https://www.intelligence.senate.gov/sites/default/files/hearings/95mkultra.pdf.

426 Project MKULTRA, The CIA'S Program of Research in Behavioral Modification, pp 39–41 and 187–188, https://www.intelligence.senate.gov/sites/default/files/hearings/95mkultra.pdf.

427 Foster, *The MKULTRA Compendium,* p 608.

428 Foster, *The MKULTRA Compendium,* p 613.

429 Foster, *The MKULTRA Compendium,* p 614.

430 Foster, *the MKULTRA Compendium,* p 607.

431 Government Interests, Method and apparatus for associative memory, US Patent 5,995,954 "This invention was made with Government support provided by the Defense Advanced Research Projects Agency, ARPA Order 6429, through Contract DAAH01-88-C-0887, issued by the U.S. Army Missile Command. The Government has certain rights in the invention."

432 Method and apparatus for associative memory, US Patent 5,995,954 http://patft.uspto.gov/netacgi/nph-Parser?Sect1=PTO1&Sect2=HITOFF&d=PALL&p=1&u=%2Fnetahtml%2FPTO%2Fsrchnum.htm&r=1&f=G&l=50&s1=5,995,954.PN.&OS=PN/5,995,954&RS=PN/5,995,954, accessed September 30, 2019.

433 David Talbot, *The Devil's Chessboard,* p 308.

434 Elizabeth Thompson, *Federal government quietly compensates daughter of brainwashing experiments victim,* https://www.cbc.ca/news/politics/cia-brainwashing-allanmemorial-mentalhealth-1.4373590, CBC News, October 26, 2017, accessed April 3, 2019.

435 Talbot, *The Devil's Chessboard,* p 305.

436 Talbot, *The Devil's Chessboard,* p 306.

437 Talbot, *The Devil's Chessboard,* p 298.

438 Talbot, *The Devil's Chessboard,* p 306.

439 Talbot, *The Devil's Chessboard,* p 307.

440   Project MKULTRA, The CIA'S Program of Research in Behavioral Modification, p 8, https://www.intelligence.senate.gov/sites/default/files/hearings/95mkultra.pdf.

441   Project MKULTRA, The CIA'S Program of Research in Behavioral Modification, p 24, https://www.intelligence.senate.gov/sites/default/files/hearings/95mkultra.pdf.

The Editors, "Spy vs. Spy's Castro Connection," *Mad Magazine*, November 29th, 2016, https://www.madmagazine.com/blog/2016/11/29/spy-vs-spys-castro-connection, accessed September 6, 2019.

442   Constance Scharff, "Neuroplasticity and Addiction Recovery," *Psychology Today*, February 05, 2013, https://www.psychologytoday.com/us/blog/ending-addiction-good/201302/neuroplasticity-and-addiction-recovery , accessed September 9, 2019.

443   Charles P. O'Brien, "Neuroplasticity in addictive disorders," *Dialogues Clin Neurosci.* 2009 Sep; 11(3): 350–353 accessed on https://www.ncbi.nlm.nih.gov/pmc/articles/PMC3181920/, accessed September 9, 2019.

444   Joyce Shaffer "Neuroplasticity and Clinical Practice: Building Brain Power for Health," *Front Psychol.* 2016; 7: 1118. Published online 2016 Jul 26. doi: 10.3389/fpsyg.2016.01118, accessed on https://www.ncbi.nlm.nih.gov/pmc/articles/PMC4960264/, accessed September 9, 2019.

445   DrugRehab.org, *Neuroplasticity And Addiction Recovery*, https://www.drugrehab.org/neuroplasticity-and-addiction-recovery/, accessed September 9, 2019.

446   *Smartphone Addiction Signs and Symptoms – Are You a Nomophobe?*, Addiction Resource, June 24th, 2019, https://addictionresource.com/addiction/technology-addiction/smartphone-addiction/smartphone-addiction-signs/, accessed August 14, 2019.

447   The National Institute for Occupational Safety and Health (NIOSH), *Lead*, https://www.cdc.gov/niosh/topics/lead/health.html, accessed November 2, 2019.

448   Iltifat Husain, MD, *Key takeaways from the American Academy of Pediatrics tablet and smartphone guidelines for children*, American Academy of Pediatrics (AAP), November 11, 2016, https://www.imedicalapps.com/2016/11/american-academy-pediatrics-tablet-smartphone-guidelines-children, accessed September 3, 2019.

449   Trevor Haynes, *Dopamine Smartphones,* Department of Neurobiology at Harvard Medical School. http://sitn.hms.harvard.edu/flash/2018/dopamine-smartphones-battle-time/, accessed July 26, 2019.

450   D. Sutoo, K. Akiyama, *Regulation of brain function by exercise*, Neu-

robiol Dis. 2003 Jun;13(1):1-14, abstract, https://www.ncbi.nlm.nih.gov/pubmed/12758062, accessed July 3, 2019.

451   David J Linden, "Exercise, pleasure and the brain," *Psychology Today*, April 21, 2011, https://www.psychologytoday.com/us/blog/the-compass-pleasure/201104/exercise-pleasure-and-the-brain, accessed August 4, 2019.

452   Robert H. Lustig, "The Hacking of the American Mind: The Science Behind the Corporate Takeover of Our Bodies and Brains," *Avery* (September 12, 2017) 352 pages.

453   August Brice, *60 Minutes on Brain Hacking: Smartphone Addiction, How to Retrain Your Brain,* April 10, 2017, https://medium.com/@TechWellness/brain-hacking-60-minutes-heres-how-to-have-power-over-your-smartphone-91651480bf9a, accessed September 13, 2019.

454   HelpGuide, *Smartphone Addiction*, https://www.helpguide.org/articles/addictions/smartphone-addiction.htm?pdf=12397, accessed July 26, 2019.

455   American Addiction Centers, *Treatment for Addiction to Smartphones* PsychGuides.com, 2019, https://www.psychguides.com/behavioral-disorders/smart-phone-addiction/, accessed August 14, 2019.

456   Susan Davis, Reviewed by Laura J. Martin, MD, *Addicted to Your Smartphone? Here's What to Do*, WebMD, 2012, https://www.webmd.com/balance/guide/addicted-your-smartphone-what-to-do, accessed August 14, 2019.

457   Royal Society for Public Health, *#StatusOfMindSocial media and young people's mental health and wellbeing*, May 2017, pp 24-26, https://www.rsph.org.uk/uploads/assets/uploaded/d125b27c-0b62-41c5-a2c0155a8887cd01.pdf , accessed September 12, 2019.

458   Justia, *Actual and Proximate Cause*, https://www.justia.com/injury/negligence-theory/actual-and-proximate-cause/, accessed July 28, 2019.

459   Anderson Cooper, *Brain Hacking,* 60 Minutes, CBS News, Jan 10, 2018, https://www.youtube.com/watch?v=awAMTQZmvPE, accessed April 6, 2019.

460   *Principles of Substance Abuse Prevention for Early Childhood,* National Institute of Drug Abuse (NIDA), https://www.drugabuse.gov/publications/principles-substance-abuse-prevention-early-childhood/chapter-1-why-early-childhood-important-to-substance-abuse-prevention#adolescent-drug-use accessed April 28, 2019.

461   HeathyChildren.org, *Parents of Young Children: Put Down Your Smartphones,* https://www.healthychildren.org/English/family-life/Media/Pages/Parents-of-Young-Children-Put-Down-Your-Smartphones.aspx,

accessed August 2, 2019.

462   Bahar Gholipour, *Gamer's Thrombosis: How Playing Too Long Could Be Deadly,* Live Science, December 10, 2013, https://www.livescience.com/41839-gamers-thrombosis.html, accessed July 1, 2019.

463   Rebecca Twomey, "Xbox addict, 20, killed by blood clot after 12-hour gaming sessions," *Daily Mail,* 6 January 2016, https://www.dailymail.co.uk/news/article-2020462/Xbox-addict-20-killed-blood-clot-12-hour-gaming-sessions.html, accessed July 1, 2019.

464   Memorandum for Secretary of Defense, Subject Experimentation Programs Conducted by the Department of Defense That Had CIA Sponsorship or Participation and That Involved to Administration to Human Subjects Intended for Mind-control or Behavior-modification Purposes, September 20, 1977, pp 7–8, https://www.esd.whs.mil/Portals/54/Documents/FOID/Reading%20Room/NCB/02-A-0846_RELEASE.pdf, accessed April 6, 2019.

465   Chapter 1: Subject Matter and Scope of Copyright, Copyright Law of the United States, Copyright.gov, https://www.copyright.gov/title17/92chap1.html#105, accessed August 15, 2019.

466   CENDI Copyright Working Group, *Frequently Asked Questions About Copyright*
Issues Affecting the U.S. Government, Published by CENDI Secretariat, Information International Associates, Inc., Oak Ridge, TN, October 2008, https://www.cendi.gov/publications/04-8copyright.html, accessed August 15, 2019.

467   Question 3.2.5, , CENDI Copyright Working Group, https://www.cendi.gov/publications/04-8copyright.html#325, accessed August 15, 2019.

468   CENDI Copyright Working Group, https://www.cendi.gov/publications/04-8copyright.html, accessed August 15, 2019.

469   Question 2.2.2, CENDI Copyright Working Group, https://www.cendi.gov/publications/04-8copyright.html#325, accessed August 15, 2019.

470   Question 2.3.2, CENDI Copyright Working Group, https://www.cendi.gov/publications/04-8copyright.html#325, accessed August 15, 2019.

471   Question 3.1.8, CENDI Copyright Working Group, https://www.cendi.gov/publications/04-8copyright.html#325, accessed August 15, 2019.

472   Question 3.2.5, CENDI Copyright Working Group, https://www.cendi.gov/publications/04-8copyright.html#325, accessed August 15, 2019.

473 Chapter 1: Subject Matter and Scope of Copyright, Copyright Law of the United States, Copyright.gov, https://www.copyright.gov/title17/92chap1.html#105, accessed August 15, 2019.

474 Section 105, Subject matter of copyright: United States Government works, Chapter 1: Subject Matter and Scope of Copyright, Copyright Law of the United States, Copyright.gov, https://www.copyright.gov/title17/92chap1.html#105, accessed August 15, 2019.

475 Section 106, Subject matter of copyright: United States Government works, Chapter 1: Subject Matter and Scope of Copyright, Copyright Law of the United States, Copyright.gov, https://www.copyright.gov/title17/92chap1.html#106, accessed August 15, 2019.

476 Section 107, Subject matter of copyright: United States Government works, Chapter 1: Subject Matter and Scope of Copyright, Copyright Law of the United States, Copyright.gov, https://www.copyright.gov/title17/92chap1.html#107, accessed August 15, 2019.

477 Richard Stim, *The 'Fair Use' Rule: When Use of Copyrighted Material Is Acceptable,* Nolo https://www.nolo.com/legal-encyclopedia/fair-use-rule-copyright-material-30100.html, accessed August 15, 2019.

478 CENDI Copyright Working Group, *Frequently Asked Questions About Copyright*
Issues Affecting the U.S. Government, Published by CENDI Secretariat, Information International Associates, Inc., Oak Ridge, TN, October 2008, https://www.cendi.gov/publications/04-8copyright.html, accessed August 15, 2019.

479 The Supreme Court, Harper & Row v. Nation Enterprises, 471 U.S. 539 (1985), https://www.law.cornell.edu/copyright/cases/471_US_539.htm, accessed August 16, 2019.

480 Richard Stim, *The 'Fair Use' Rule: When Use of Copyrighted Material Is Acceptable,* Nolo https://www.nolo.com/legal-encyclopedia/fair-use-rule-copyright-material-30100.html, accessed August 15, 2019.

481 Fair Use, Digital Media Law Project, http://www.dmlp.org/legal-guide/fair-use, accessed August 15, 2019.

482 Richard Stim, *The 'Fair Use' Rule: When Use of Copyrighted Material Is Acceptable,* Nolo https://www.nolo.com/legal-encyclopedia/fair-use-rule-copyright-material-30100.html, accessed August 15, 2019.

CPSIA information can be obtained
at www.ICGtesting.com
Printed in the USA
BVHW031446060420
57699JBV00008B/45